PRAISE FOR *DU*

Few people see the reality that a child in the foster care system faces. *Dumpster Doll* gives you an inside glimpse of such a reality. As you read, you may tell yourself that this doesn't really happen, that in America, children are not subjected to such abuse and neglect. You are wrong. *Dumpster Doll* gives you a chance to open your eyes and glimpse what children in the system go through and how they got there. You may be uncomfortable and I hope that you are. It is my sincere hope that *Dumpster Doll* provokes you to do something in your own community to help children.

—Crystal Morgan, attorney, child advocate,
founder of Fostering Love, a 501(c)(3) non-profit
benefitting foster children

Dumpster Doll is truly heartwarming, depressing, and inspiring... Michelle's ability to recall events in her life and put the reader in her place is a talent that not enough of us have. I admit my eyes teared up a number of times. Her experiences recalled to my mind a number of the more horrible case reports I read while representing the Department in Arizona for four years. Some may think these experiences are exaggerated, but my background tells me that, if anything, Michelle has left out some of the horrors. This is an important book, and I look forward to reading the next one.

— J. Kevin Earp, former children's services attorney,
author of *The Marcus Lear Mysteries*

Praise for *Dumpster Doll*

I was riveted. This book brought up thoughts I've often had about "reunification." I've worked with families in which the parents were drug abusers and not capable of taking care of themselves much less their children. I've seen all the systems work like mad to give services to the parents so the kids can be reunited with their parents (again) and I've thought, *Should we be doing this?* I've seen as many as five reunification attempts in some families. The only way it ends for the kid is when he/she turns eighteen and ages out of the system. Some parents will never be capable of actually being "good" parents. This book should be required reading for all!

—Lynn West, Former Chief Executive Officer at
TCN Behavioral Health Services in Greene County, Ohio

Dumpster Doll

The Early Years

Michelle Mays & Michelle Moone

CONTENTS

This book is dedicated to the discarded and neglected, and to those with hearts big enough to take them in and give them a loving home.

Foreword
MICHELLE MOONE:
CO-AUTHOR

This is not my story. I am simply an instrument used to give someone else a voice. Yes, we are both named Michelle, and yes, this book is written in the first person, but this book is about my best friend, Michelle Mays, the dumpster doll.

We've collaborated on this project because Michelle has always wanted to share her story, and it's certainly worth telling, but the task of writing your own life story, especially one that deals with traumatic and heavy topics, is a little like trying to drink from a fire hose.

Dumpster Doll: The Early Years is a remarkable account of Michelle Mays' first twelve years. Reminiscent of a Greek tragedy, she endured sexual abuse, a near fatal accident, and abandonment. Michelle persisted and, with the support of some wonderful people, has leveraged her life experiences to grow and serve as a shining example that it is possible to overcome the past and choose happiness over bitterness and despair.

Michelle and I met in 2006 while working in the same department of a telecommunications company. My first impression of her was one of a confident and cheerful go-getter; Michelle's effervescent personality won her many friends. In short order, Michelle began to reveal some momentous details of her personal history. Little did I know that what she shared with me barely scratched the surface. It was clear that Michelle's aim was to one day share her compelling story with the world, not to say, "Hey, look at me, don't you feel sorry for me because of all that I've been through?" Michelle's overarching desire is to share her story and offer hope and courage to those who are in despair from similar experiences and find themselves simply surviving; to demonstrate that the kindness and compassion of others can go a long way toward improving the lives of such souls; and to pay homage to these guardians of the discarded and neglected. She wants to prove that what happens to you doesn't have to define you. Life experiences are merely brushstrokes in the beautiful portrait that is you. Some brushstrokes are whisper-thin and others are bold and heavy; it takes all of them to produce each person's rich and vibrant portrait. Deep down, we possess the fortitude to rise above horrible situations and succeed; success, after all, is the best revenge. It's not an easy path, and Michelle is the first one to admit that she struggles with demons. But she channels what she has gleaned from surrogates and mentors and finds the strength to propel herself forward using the momentum from large and small victories—even at such a tender age, we get to see Michelle developing her character and establishing her voice.

Michelle and I launched ourselves into the journey of writing her story. We began tracing her family tree and chronicling birth order and family history over a BBQ dinner. From there, we settled into a routine that Michelle aptly named "Friday Write Night, Saturday Café." Our writing sessions started as we finished dinner on Friday nights. Then we'd work all night and into the morning, ending with a bite to eat at a local breakfast spot. This schedule evolved many times over as life certainly would not wait for this book to be written.

Reading *Dumpster Doll: The Early Years* will remind you of the fragility of life, the strength of the human spirit, and the supremacy of God's infinite and unwavering love and mercy—even if we choose to push it away.

Preface
MICHELLE MAYS:
THE DUMPSTER DOLL

Walking into a courthouse has always felt strange to me. Something about the building is so cold and uninviting, yet familiar. Do they design the buildings unnecessarily large and hollow to intimidate the accused? I can't imagine it makes the victims feel any better.

Hearing my footsteps echo throughout the large corridor as I walked over to my family left me with a feeling of uneasiness. However it made me feel, I was forty-two and I'd dealt with worse. I could swallow this feeling deep into my gut and be supportive for my family members who needed me.

As I came to the second floor, I saw them on a heavy wooden bench to the right, whispering so their voices wouldn't echo throughout the building. Seated there were my mother's sisters and Uncle Mike, Aunt Mary's husband. Coming in closer, I saw my cousins standing against the edge of the stone banister that surrounded the large hole in the middle of the room where you could see down to the first floor. I swallowed the feeling of intimidation again and gave hugs to all, as I had not seen some of these people in years.

It hadn't even been a week since I saw Andy's post online, ranting and raving about Uncle Mike being a rapist. It was such a long post that I hadn't finished reading. Immediately I thought, *I need to call Aunt Mary and find out what is going on.* My aunt was crying so hard that she could barely explain what had happened. I just wanted to give her a hug and take her pain away. I could feel her pain deep down in my chest. I understood the important part of the conversation—her husband was in jail for molesting Andy's teenage stepdaughter. Aunt Mary just couldn't fathom the possibility of this being true. She was in shock, and I honestly couldn't believe what I was hearing myself. Uncle Mike was such a funny and hardworking guy who seemed to love his family and did lots of family activities with them. I immediately felt I needed to get both sides of the story, and I called Andy.

Aunt Mary adopted Andy when he was three years old. Even though I've had to call him my cousin for the past thirty-two years, he is my brother by blood. I raised him his first three years, and so I feel a maternal instinct to try and protect him. He had spent some time in prison for violent behavior, so I wanted to talk to him and make sure he didn't overreact and do anything that would put him back there.

I listened to Andy sob as he told me about his stepdaughter's account of the situation, and that it had been going on for years. I wanted to give him a hug and take his pain away. I could feel his pain deep down in my chest. I honestly didn't know what to say; if it were my kid, someone would be dead or hanging on by a thread for dear life. I obviously couldn't give Andy that advice for fear of him acting on it. I let him know that this was never an easy thing for a family to deal with, and how they reacted could affect his stepdaughter for the rest of her life. I advised him to be supportive and talk to a counselor to discuss how to deal with this.

Scanning the corridor of the courthouse, I located Andy directly opposite of where I was standing, about 500 feet away on the other side of the hole. Suddenly the hole felt like it was trying to say something else. Like the void we had felt our entire lives with a big empty space separating us from our family. It was almost as if I needed to pick a side to sit on, as if I were saying, *I am only here for this person.* Andy was sitting with his wife, her two kids from a previous relationship, and their beautiful little girl they had together. This little girl was the spitting image of Andy when he was three years old. It took me back for a moment, seeing a little blond three-year-old with a snotty nose crying because he was hungry, but I had buried that time and quickly brought myself back to the present. I couldn't allow myself to go there for fear of not being able to control what I might say.

I have managed to keep my wits about me (for the most part) all these years raising my boys to be successful, hard-working adults by burying what has happened and just trying like hell not to repeat any of what my siblings and I went through. I only wish I could have helped my brothers deal with it like I have. I'm not saying how I have dealt with the helping of shit-stew I have been served is the best method for everyone, but it worked for me.

I walked over to hug them all. I wanted them to know that I was there for everyone hurting and didn't want to take sides. Why did there have to be sides? I couldn't understand why everyone was so separated in this large room. During hard times, a family should try to stick together, right? If for no other reason than so the children can learn that they don't have to go through a tragedy or hardship alone.

Andy and his family started following me back over to where our aunts and cousins were sitting. Immediately they were stopped midway by some of the family sitting on Uncle Mike's side and were told not to come over. The kids started crying because they didn't understand why they were being shunned by the rest of the family. They returned to the other side of the hole in the family, so accurately represented by the gaping hole in the floor.

I started hearing the aunts and cousins saying things like, "How dare they come over here? They shouldn't be coming over here. They will only make this worse." I felt a deep burning in my gut that became hotter and hotter and rose like lava up through my chest until it came out of my mouth. Everything that I had buried for so many years was erupting, and I couldn't stop it. The hairs on my arms stood at attention, and like a teapot reaching its boiling point, I screamed.

"You all have *no* idea what we went through. You have no idea what our mother did or what we had to endure. None of you protected us or were there for us, and now it is a vicious cycle repeating itself."

The look of shock on their faces said it all. No, they didn't have any idea what we went through. I had never talked about it with any of them. I always assumed that if I didn't repeat the past—if I put on a smile and stayed strong for others when they needed it—that everything would be okay. Is it, though? Their silence was deafening. Perhaps my silence about what happened to me kept everyone in the family oblivious to the signs they should have noticed. Something wasn't right with the teenage girl and her relationship with her grandfather, and it could have been caught much earlier or not have happened at all. How could I have helped prevent this?

I have written stories in school with bits and pieces of my experiences for a paper here and there to demonstrate a certain subject. My teachers and professors—as far back as my senior year in high school to just recently in my psychology class in college—have told me I needed to write my story. My response was always, "I will one day." In the back of my mind I always thought, *Who am I that anyone would care to read my story? I am not famous. I am doing just fine and I don't need to rehash all that ugliness.* It wasn't until that day in the courthouse that I understood why I needed to write my story.

This story isn't for me.

This story is for you, dear friend, if you were forced or coerced into a sexual act by a trusted family member or friend. This story is for all the parents who aren't sure how to recognize the symptoms of sexual abuse.

This story is for you if you've ever had a drug-addicted parent. This story is for the parents who think that kids don't notice when you drink or take drugs. Guess what, they do.

This story is for you, abandoned child who feels like you aren't wanted or worth a pot to piss in. This story is for all loving families with hearts big enough to take in a stranger's child, even if only for a short time. A short time spent receiving some love is better than no love at all.

This story is for you if you are unsure of yourself and feel the need to please others before pursuing your own happiness.

This story is for you if you judge others based on their appearance or what they own. You never know what their back-story may be or how you could cause further damage.

This story is for all the people with the means to help but who aren't sure how to help or who needs the help. Maybe you're unsure if it will even make a difference.

Believe me when I say, it does.

Before There Was Me

Some people say that destiny chooses who we will end up with, while others talk about love at first sight. There are also contradictory clichés like "birds of a feather flock together" and "opposites attract." Whatever force sparked their attraction and drew them together, the fact remains: Mom and Dad met and fell in love.

Dad was raised in Lebanon, Ohio, as one of five sons in a devout Evangelical household. Despite his parents' better judgment, Dad's dream of moving to San Francisco and becoming a hippy was realized after he graduated from high school. It was the mid-sixties and the lure of the psychedelic counterculture of Haight-Ashbury was irresistible to him. At the age of seventeen and armed with his high school diploma and his souped-up '57 Chevy, Dad and two of his buddies made their way out west.

Having spent all their money just to reach The City by the

Bay, they capitalized on Dad's modified car by participating in drag races and living off their cash winnings. While they won a fair number of races, they still had to make do on a tight budget. Dad and his friends soon learned that money does not grow on trees, and they often survived on meager meals of snack food.

One afternoon, as they were parked at a grocery store enjoying their lunch of saltines and Coke while leaning up against their car—now meal ticket—they saw three sets of long, slender legs that had been kissed by the California sun. The girls wore short shorts and flowing halter tops. They had flowers in their hair and they embodied the essence of San Francisco hippies. The girls had a rented house with four other girls but had no car. Brokering a deal, the girls agreed to trade space in their home in exchange for the car and chauffeur service by Dad and his friends.

Dad was enjoying his freedom in California with like-minded hippies. The counterculture celebrated peace and love while exploring new horizons of sexual promiscuity and recreational drugs, as the Grateful Dead, Janis Joplin, Jimi Hendrix, and others provided the era's celebrated soundtrack.

Meanwhile, back in Ohio, Dad's draft notification came in the mail. After he got a call from Grandma, Dad began making arrangements to sell his car and buy a ticket back to Ohio. Soon after his return, he was on his way to the jungles of Vietnam.

By the age of twenty, Dad had graduated from a very strict and sheltered religious upbringing, lived the devil-may-care hippy lifestyle in San Francisco, fought for America in savage jungles halfway around the world, made lifelong friends and lost some of them in those very jungles, was exposed to the nefarious effects of Agent Orange, and suffered post-traumatic stress disorder. When he returned from Vietnam, factory work was the only worthwhile option for veterans, so he secured a full-time job with an appliance company.

Mom grew up in Dayton, Ohio, as one of eleven children. Her father was an entrepreneur and inventor. He owned a small chain of grocery stores and held several patents. His first wife bore him a son, but when she abandoned them he married her sister, Frances. All outward appearances indicated a happy home life, but when he left for work, Frances would lock all eleven children in the basement for the day. She would send down food for lunch—usually bread and bologna—but other than that, the children were left to their own devices. It wasn't until their dad's nightly return, when they heard the car door shut, that Frances would unlock the basement door and call the kids back upstairs. It was clearly understood that no one was allowed to reveal Frances' willful neglect. Undoubtedly, all of the children spent their evenings clinging to their father, as this was the only parental compassion they received.

When Mom was fourteen years old, Frances introduced her to the sordid world of neighborhood dive bars where she encouraged her to drink, smoke, and flirt with men old enough to be her father. Clearly, this wretched excuse for a role model is where Mom's horrific parenting style was developed.

Mom and Dad met in a bowling alley in Lebanon, Ohio, and began dating shortly after that. Dad was aware of Mom's substance abuse problems, but the heart wants what the heart wants. They married and had many discussions about how to build their future. With Mom pregnant and real adult responsibilities bearing down on Dad, he decided that re-enlisting in the Marines would be the best way to support his family.

Just like concentric ripples in still water when a stone is tossed in, the far-reaching effects of neglect and abuse continue from generation to generation. It takes a conscious decision and a strong will to break the cycle.

Dad in the Marines, 1968

Mom, Louie, and Dad, 1973

Mom, 1972

Mom pregnant with me, 1973

Taboo

It was 1977. Jimmy Carter was president, minimum wage was $2.30, Elvis died, *Star Wars* was a huge box-office success, and Seattle Slew won the Kentucky Derby. Any one of these or a million other things that year undoubtedly served as the guiding force behind the lives of Americans, but none of these affected me. I was not a lifelong DC politician, nor was I trying to keep my family afloat on minimum wage; musical icons, cinema blockbusters, or sports championships had not yet dominated my interest. I was a four-year-old little girl in Waynesville, Ohio.

Childhood memories tend to be foggy and disjointed. We have the tendency to recall only bits and pieces of any given event. However, some memories are so intricately woven into the tapestry of our being that we cannot escape them, no matter how hard we try.

We lived in a trailer park about five miles outside the city limits of Waynesville. My nuclear family consisted of Dad, a United States Marine stationed in Japan; Mom; and two brothers: Louie, two years older than me, and Eric, still an infant. We had settled in Waynesville so Mom would have the support of her father and some of her ten siblings while Dad was away on active duty. The trailer was very basic with white aluminum and burgundy trim. It was parked on a simple concrete slab, and there was no attempt to improve its curb appeal with flower boxes at the windows or landscaping of any kind. We had three microscopic bedrooms, one bathroom, a living room, and a kitchen.

Looking back, I'm sure the trailer's size offered little more than suffocating, claustrophobic comfort, especially when we were all home. But for those who look for life's silver linings, maintaining impeccable housekeeping certainly would have been easier in this tin can of a home than in a sprawling ranch or two-story house in the suburbs.

The confines of a mobile home didn't bother me in the least; I didn't have anything to compare it to and everything seems big to a four-year-old. My needs were met. I had a place to sleep and food to eat, and even though it was small, Louie and I still found nooks and crannies for hide-and-seek. In fact, the one vivid memory that still stands out is the distinct smell of Pine-Sol; this was Mom's favorite cleaning agent.

Even today, when I get a whiff of that stuff, I'm not

magically transported to a North Carolina pine forest like their commercial touts. Instead, I am psychologically summoned back to 1977, to that trailer park, to that mobile home, in Waynesville, Ohio.

When the weather was nice we played outside—hide-and-seek and tag when Louie was with me. When I was alone, I played with Barbie dolls or found something else to entertain myself. I especially loved to ride my pink and purple Big Wheel; I liked watching the plastic streamers that hung from the ends of the handlebars. They would flap and flow as a low-tech indicator of my speed.

One day, pedaling through the lanes that curved through the trailer park, I heard the distant sound of a car approaching. I knew enough to get out of the way, so I steered the clunky plastic toy to the side of the lane and into the lawn area that was peppered with bare spots and dandelions. Disco music escaped through the open car windows as the driver approached and rolled to a stop near me. It was Aunt Barb. She was fun, she always took time to play with me, and I really loved her. Excited to see her, I abandoned the Big Wheel right where I was and ran inside to give Aunt Barb a big hug. "Are you here to play with us?" I asked as the screen door slammed behind me. I knew Mom hated the loud crash of the screen door as it banged against the door frame, especially when she was otherwise occupied and the noise startled her, but I was excited that I would have a new playmate for the evening.

"No, your mom and I are going out tonight. Uncle Jeff will be here soon, and he'll stay with you." Since Dad was away on extended leave, Mom always needed to arrange for someone to watch us if she wanted to go out.

As hard as I try to remember anything good or fun about Uncle Jeff, nothing comes to mind. I'm sure he was an average eighteen-year-old; he probably liked pizza and beer with his friends, Friday night football, and maybe an impromptu game of basketball. The truth is, I just don't have these kinds of memories about him.

I watched and mimicked as Mom and Aunt Barb preened in the bathroom mirror. They were fixing their long hair. My long blond hair was stringy and knotted. Powdered blush made their cheeks rosy. My cheeks were rosy too, evidence of my youth and a full day of playing outside.

Uncle Jeff arrived just as they were finishing their primping. On their way out the door, Mom gave me and Louie a quick squeeze, kisses on our cheeks, and instructions for the evening: "I want you to pick up around here. Wipe down the table and counter in the kitchen, clean the bathroom, vacuum, and dust."

My very first traumatic memory is of Uncle Jeff sneaking into the bathroom while I was in there. His tall frame towered over me like a tree with shaggy, curly red hair. There I was, sitting on the toilet with my dress pulled up and panties down around my knees. My legs dangled because my tiny feet were nowhere near able to reach the floor. Uncle Jeff pulled his erect penis out of his pants and put it in my face. I could easily see fluid on the tip, and I protested. My innocent little voice cried out, "Eww, there's pee on it!"

In a soft and calming tone, he reassured me that it was not pee, and he continued coaxing me to touch it with my hands and mouth. Sensing that he wouldn't let me go otherwise, I finally summoned the courage to wrap my tiny hands around it, and then he told me to lick it like a lollipop. Even at my tender age of four, I instinctively knew that this was horribly wrong and against nature. With little effort, Uncle Jeff ejaculated all over my mouth and face. My four-year-old face that should have been smothered with kisses from Mommy and Daddy, or covered with sticky cupcake frosting and ice cream, instead had been defiled with semen from a teenage sexual predator who also happened to be my uncle.

Afterward, I clearly remember straining on my tiptoes to reach the sink so I could wash my face. My reflection looked back at me from the mirror. Physically, I looked the same: long snow-white hair and big blue eyes. But emotionally, I was forever changed. If only it were as easy to wash away the memory and shame, watching as they swirled down the drain with soap bubbles and seed.

Louie stood in the hallway as I left the bathroom. Had he heard my pleas through the bathroom door? Did he know what had happened to me? Had it ever happened to him too? My soul filled with disgrace and filth from the event, and I wanted to hide forever. This encounter in the bathroom with my uncle left such an indelible mark on my spirit that I was terrified to use the bathroom when a man was in the trailer. Instead, I would opt to wet myself and face Mom's wrath.

Unwilling to assume the domestic role and do housework, Mom would assign chores for us kids to complete in her absence. We would rotate the tasks: vacuuming the carpet, sweeping the kitchen floor, and dusting. I distinctly remember wanting vacuum duty. I liked to navigate the vacuum just so to make perfectly straight tracks in the carpet—visual evidence of my hard work.

One particular day, Uncle Jeff ordered Louie to vacuum so he could take me to his room to satisfy his perverted needs. Just like before, he invaded my personal space. This time, Uncle Jeff put the tip of his shaft in my mouth. He then thrust his hips, causing his penis to plunge deeper into my mouth and ram the back of my throat. My gag reflex was triggered, and I threw up in my mouth and then swallowed it. I didn't know what was happening or why, but I remember thinking that I couldn't wait for Dad to get home from Japan. I knew that he would take care of the situation when he learned what was happening to me.

My last memory of Uncle Jeff's assault on my innocence happened in the car while delivering weekly ads to neighborhood homes in the area. Mom and her brother would each take a car and a kid. They would steer the car along the curb, and it was our job to roll up the weekly ads and slide them into the plastic bins that were always mounted on the posts right below the mailboxes.

Uncle Jeff chose me as his ride-along companion for the day, and I threw myself to the floor in a violent temper tantrum. Kicking and screaming, I was desperate to avoid another experience with my abuser. The thought of being alone in the car with my uncle meant only one thing to me: I was about to be subjected to his deviant urges.

Mom had no patience with my tantrum, nor did she care to learn the reason that fueled it. She yanked my crumpled body off the floor, ignored my tear-streaked cheeks, spanked me, and then, to reinforce the dominance a parent has over a child, she demanded that I ride with Uncle Jeff as added punishment, while she took Louie with her.

After I resigned myself to the fact that I was doomed to be my uncle's plaything, we were on our way. In the car he made me pull my pants and panties down. While steering the car with one hand, he reached over to fondle me with his other hand. Anyone on the outside looking in would never imagine the incestuous scene taking place. Fear struck us both when a man from the neighborhood approached the car on the passenger side. Uncle Jeff panicked and tossed a bunch of the ads on my lap to conceal the fact that I was essentially nude from the waist down. This man was none the wiser and stood there with his head poked in the open window chatting with my uncle. I sat on the passenger side of the car, half buried in weekly grocery ads, staring up into his face and hoping and praying that he wouldn't notice what was really going on inside my personal hell.

I once tried to escape that hell. A few days after the incident in the car with my uncle, I was riding the school bus home from my half-day of pre-school. I knew that Mom wasn't home, and Louie wouldn't be back from his full day of school until later. That meant that I would be home alone with Uncle Jeff. The school bus was filled with the usual sounds of children—chatter, giggles, and the excitement of returning home from preschool to share all the fun that preschool offers with eagerly awaiting moms. But as the miles passed and we bounced along in the bus, I was filled with the dreaded anticipation of what could possibly be waiting for me on the other side of our trailer's front door. I just couldn't face another encounter with Uncle Jeff, so I decided right then and there to make my escape.

I convinced a little girl from pre-school who was riding the bus to get off at my stop and run away with me. We had no grandiose plan to reach the big city or join the circus. I just needed to get away, and I didn't want to do it alone, so we walked…and walked. It felt like we walked forever, and we made it as far as the covered bridge. As we approached the bridge, we passed a man and woman who were sitting on their front porch. They called us over and offered us something to drink. Unsuspicious and thirsty, we eagerly drank and were thankful for the brief rest. But before we knew it, the police showed up. We had been betrayed by our cordial hosts! Their hospitality was just a ruse to lure us to them so they had time to summon the police to come and take us home. I remember wishing that they would allow me to live with them. I wished they could be my new parents—at least until Dad got home from Japan.

As the police pulled up to our trailer and I climbed out of their cruiser with my fruit-punch moustache, Mom put on an Oscar-worthy performance. Even though I doubt she noticed that I had been missing, she feigned genuine concern for my safety and expressed pseudo gratitude that I had been returned home safely. Her insincerity was recognizable only to me. Once the policemen left and we were back inside, she spared no strength in the spanking I received. Mom's large hands landed swiftly on my backside with loud thuds. Each blow jostled me to my core. As bad as this punishment was, the alternative of an afternoon with my uncle would have been much worse.

Me, three years old, 1976

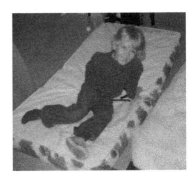

Me, four years old, 1977

The Mom I Knew

Mom's other ten siblings were nowhere near as formidable as she was. But even at my young age, I was aware that she wasn't like other mommies. She valued chain smoking, drinking beer, and flipping through magazines or reading trashy romance novels over engaging us in play, reading to us, or showering us with love and affection. Mom had a propensity to leave us at home while she sought the company of men or tried to score a deal that would leave her strung out on the couch for hours at a time.

Even when Mom was home with us, she failed at being a mother. She would drink herself into a drunken stupor and lay sprawled out on the green Naugahyde couch, unable to function. One time, I remember our mean little Chihuahua, Snoopy, no longer able to resist the sight of her arm dangling off the side of the couch. He wandered over and chomped on her hand. Mom woke up in a blind rage, and before I knew what was happening, she scooped him up with one hand and launched him across the room. Snoopy was airborne for a quick moment before slamming into the wall. That was the Mom I knew when no one was watching.

Not only did Mom negatively impact the lives of her husband and her children, she also managed to devastate the life of her younger sister Linda and the lives of Linda's son and daughter, Johnny and Jennifer. Aunt Linda was raising her two small children on her own while struggling with a full-time job and trying to put herself through nursing school. Mom offered Aunt Linda a sense of security by allowing them to move in with us so she could watch the kids while Aunt Linda was at work and school. Mom required that Aunt Linda hand over her paycheck each week, which left her incapable of saving for her own independence.

To add insult to injury, Mom abused Johnny and Jennifer. It wasn't until a neighbor heard a child crying and came to investigate that the abuse was discovered. The neighbor lady entered the trailer when no one answered the front door. She found the two kids home alone. Johnny, still just a toddler, was sitting in a bathtub filled with ice water. Having spent at least an hour in the frigid water, he was shivering and turning blue. It was discovered that Mom employed this technique as punishment for whatever transgression Johnny committed. This neighbor rescued Johnny and Jennifer and harbored them in her trailer until Aunt Linda came home.

Already burning the proverbial candle at both ends, Aunt Linda was still having a difficult time staying afloat, and this was the straw that broke the camel's back. She was doing everything she thought was right for herself and her kids: working full time to provide for them, going to school to ensure a promising future, and even moving in with us to save on living expenses. Devastated by Mom's deliberate neglect and abuse and left with no other viable options, Aunt Linda made the painful decision that the best option for her children was to put them up for adoption. As agonizing as this decision was, it was made in their best interest, and Aunt Linda saw to it that Johnny and Jennifer were adopted together. She saw this injustice perpetrated by Mom as the ultimate betrayal, and thus she ended her relationship with Mom.

During this time, Aunt Mary was also putting herself through nursing school. She was a fun-spirited seventeen-year-old with long red hair and blue eyes. She always called us hon, and she was so fun to hang out with. Aunt Mary would frequently stop by the trailer to check on us on her way home from nursing school. She knew Mom was alone with the three of us and was well aware of her devil-may-care approach to childcare. It was commonplace for Aunt Mary to find our refrigerator empty except for beer and us home alone eating the only thing available—white bread with sugar sprinkled on it. To compensate for Mom's complete lack of any maternal instinct or sense of duty, Aunt Mary would regularly bring us groceries. She did her best to cultivate enjoyable memories for us, and in the summer she would take us to Cowan Lake for an afternoon of splashing and swimming. This was such a nice mini-vacation, and we looked forward to this time away from our reality.

On the way home, Aunt Mary would treat us to ice cream cones. We felt like royalty as we licked the melting sweetness and belted out the Beach Boys' anthem to summer, "Fun, Fun, Fun," from the back of her convertible. It was on these hot summer afternoons that we felt like all-American kids, thanks to Aunt Mary.

Mom's sisters did their best to provide some nurturing comfort and stability in our lives. Their compassion and maternal instincts soothed three little kids who were starved for it. Unfortunately, it didn't last long. Mom and Barb had a falling out, so Aunt Barb stopped coming around. Aunt Linda obviously distanced herself after what happened with Johnny and Jennifer. And Aunt Mary was a great temporary surrogate, but only as a stopgap. She did the best she could, but she was also committed to nursing school and she had her own life to live. In the end, it was just us with Mom.

Me, Louie, and Eric, 1978

Hello...Goodbye

Dad's year in Japan was finally over, and he got to come home. I can only imagine Dad's eagerness to return back to the States and to his family that he hadn't seen in a year. He walked into our "home-sweet-home" to find that another man had moved in. Furious, Dad threw him out and promised to kick his butt if he ever caught him around Mom again. Now that he was home, Dad was hearing all kinds of stories about Mom: her drinking and partying, how promiscuous she was, and how Aunt Mary had stepped in to ensure we were cared for. His brothers, cousins, and friends were more than happy to provide updates. He even heard gossip from his barber and the guy at the gas station. It was a small town and people talked. None of this came as a huge surprise to Dad, just a bitter disappointment. Fed up, he threatened to leave Mom if she continued down her current path. Dad even consulted an attorney and began making plans to divorce Mom and sue for custody.

By now Mom's father had passed on, and she had all but alienated herself from her siblings. Ohio had nothing and no one to offer her, so she vowed to clean up her act and move with us to the Marine base of Camp Lejeune, North Carolina. It wasn't long before we packed up and moved. I used this move as a new beginning. I never brought up the abuse I received at my uncle's hands; the shame was too great. I was ready to put it all behind me and have a normal family atmosphere. Plus, I feared if I said anything, Dad would kill him and go to jail, leaving us alone with Mom once again.

This fresh start renewed Dad's determination to get Mom clean and sober, especially since she'd announced that—surprise!—she was pregnant again. This news was exciting for me and I was hoping for a baby sister, somebody I could play dolls with and dress up like a baby doll.

The move to North Carolina was an easy one; we didn't have a lot so we traveled light. When we arrived at our newly assigned home in Camp Lejeune, I couldn't believe my eyes. Our new house, a three-bedroom duplex, was like a palace compared to the trailer where we had been living. Mom and Dad's room was at the end of the hall near the bathroom and the bedroom that Louie and Eric shared. My room, which I would eventually share with Gayle, my new baby sister, was off the hall closer to the living room. Mom kept her cedar hope chest in the hall right outside her bedroom. Every time I passed by, its woody scent transported me to an enchanted forest. I once asked Mom why she called it a hope chest, and she explained that it was where she kept all her hopes and treasures. I assumed she was referring to the family photo albums that were stored inside and never gave it another thought.

We weren't quite like the *Leave it to Beaver* family, but we did have some fun times. I really do think that Mom and Dad made a true effort to rebuild our family. I remember Mom making pancakes for us on Saturday mornings, and she would be in the kitchen cooking dinner when Dad came home for the day.

Every night, Louie and I would argue about which one of us got to unlace Dad's combat boots while he sat in his large recliner chair and relaxed from a hard day's work. Trying to keep our jealousy from escalating, Dad would assure us that we each could take a boot. This should have alleviated the nightly sibling rivalry, but we didn't want to share Dad with each other.

Eric was about two years old, and he wanted to join in on the fun, too. Louie wanted to grow up and be like Dad, and I just reveled in being his little princess. "Come on, let's dance!" Dad would bellow as he turned on his favorite Bob Seger record and began to sing, "*Just take those old records off the shelf...*" Still in his camouflage fatigues, Dad and I would cut a rug in the living room as Bob jammed on the record player. Other times Dad would play his Hollywood Argyles record with the song "Alley Oop." That was my favorite, because Dad would strut about the living room like an orangutan, swinging his arms back and forth in time with the beat. What a sight we must have been as we giggled and followed behind him mimicking his actions. We surely looked like little monkeys following their monkey papa in the jungle. Our nightly ritual ended with us brushing our teeth and Dad ushering us off to bed. He would kneel at the foot of our beds with us and recite this bedtime prayer:

> *Now I lay me down to sleep,*
> *I pray the Lord my soul to keep.*
> *If I should die before I wake,*
> *I pray the Lord my soul to take.*

Mostly it was good times, but we still had our share of drama. Dad would lose his temper occasionally, which was exacerbated by his extreme PTSD. What might have been a stern warning or a swat on the behind in the average family, easily intensified to a full-on domestic violence situation courtesy of PTSD.

When our behavior actually did justify one of Dad's whippings, he would taunt us with the knowledge that ten lashes were on the way. As he removed his brown leather belt, snapped it, and then bent us over the end of his bed, he would always reassure us that this was going to hurt him more than us. Was that supposed to make us feel better?! As much as we hated these whippings, somewhere deep in our being we knew these were punishments we deserved.

One such episode started with a sideways glance from me to Louie, which evolved to a funny face, then a poke, and then a shove. Before long, we were engaged in a full-fledged, good old-fashioned pillow fight. The sounds of gleeful giggling were punctuated with dull thumps when the pillow hit just right, and "oomph" as we absorbed the momentum of the pillow.

Yes, we had probably been warned about the risk of breaking something, but sometimes you just can't stop yourself—pillow fights are just too much fun. Eventually the inevitable happened, and one of us accidentally hit and broke the ceiling light. The glass dome that covered the light bulb and the bulb itself broke and fell to the floor. Tiny shards of glass showered down on us in the now-dark room. In an instant, our giggling stopped and we both gasped in horror. We didn't have to guess what would happen next.

Dad immediately flew into a rage, and in the heat of the moment, he took off his belt and began whipping Louie with it. Each strike was harder than the last. The only sounds came from the whoosh of the leather belt slicing through the air and Dad, swearing and broadcasting his fury, which was unreasonable and irrational. Louie knew better than to try to evade Dad or even make a peep. This would have only added fuel to the fire that was Dad's rage.

The crime certainly didn't fit the punishment. Louie's beating was so intense that he soiled himself. He sat in the bathtub, visibly distraught but half succeeding at maintaining his composure. He desperately didn't want Dad to see him cry. Dad came in and barked, "What are you upset about? I'm not done with you yet, boy." I stayed in the bathroom with Louie as an expression of solidarity. I felt so bad for him because even though I was equally culpable, I received no punishment. Looking back, I'm sure Dad's PTSD was triggered by the loud explosive sound when the glass dome hit the floor and shattered. He undoubtedly had a flashback to the jungles of Vietnam and the horrific experiences of war. I really can't begin to imagine the sights, sounds, smells, and feelings he experienced on a daily basis while there.

Another episode occurred when Louie and I engaged in a classic childhood rite of passage. We would get up before anyone else and stealthily tiptoe out to the living room to watch Saturday morning cartoons. With bleary eyes and bed heads, we sat just a few feet from the enormous color TV that was built right into its own boxy wooden frame. The volume was turned down so low that it was barely audible, but we watched cartoons like it was our job.

One morning we were so engrossed in our cartoons that we didn't hear anything else going on in the house until without warning, we heard Dad's angry voice shouting from the kitchen. "What the fuck?! Isn't anyone watching Eric?" As if he were riding a wave in the ocean, Dad's ferocity carried him to the living room where he picked up his large reclining chair and slammed it back to the ground. We were flabbergasted. What was he talking about? Eric had been sound asleep when Louie left their bedroom.

Sheepishly, Louie and I went into the kitchen to find a dozen smashed eggs in the middle of the floor, and there, in the middle of the mess, sat two-year-old Eric. He appeared as innocuous as the eye of a hurricane—calm and peaceful, but surrounded all around by his own damage and devastation. Hurricane Eric wore nothing but a diaper and a goofy grin that publicized his pure joy. Raw egg dripped from his blond curls and onto his face, then down the front of his body. His rolls of baby fat were covered in golden yolk, slippery translucent slop, and jaggedly sharp eggshells.

When he looked up from his masterpiece and saw me and Louie looking in horror at him and the destroyed kitchen, he simply giggled and squealed as he kicked his plump legs and clapped his chubby little hands. Each kick and clap sent raw egg splattering back on him and the rest of the kitchen.

Judging from the state of the disaster zone, Eric had thrown eggs at the ceiling and used the refrigerator and cabinets as target practice. Louie and I mourned what could have been a peaceful Saturday and a delicious breakfast, as we slid through the kitchen and started to clean up while Dad was having his outburst in the living room.

Mom was also aware of Dad's tendency to fly off the handle. She once spared Louie from what would otherwise have been a guaranteed beating. Louie and I were playing barber shop, and I was pretending to cut Louie's hair. I used my fingers as imaginary scissors and imitated the scissor action sound as I "cut" his hair. When it was my turn in the barber chair, I sat confidently as my stylist, Louie, went to work on my hair. I could feel Louie lift my long blond locks, which fell to the middle of my back, and "cut" my hair. He even duplicated the scissor sound with amazing accuracy. Mom came around the corner from the kitchen and shrieked like she had just seen a mouse. What she saw, and what I came to discover, was that Louie hadn't grasped the concept of pretend. Instead, he'd taken the scissors from Dad's desk and literally cut my hair. There, on the floor right next to Louie's feet, was a handful of my flaxen mane. Louie had indeed cut my hair right at chin level. With no other options, Mom had to cut the rest of my hair to even it out.

We all worried about what Dad would say when he saw my new style. Dad's Pentecostal upbringing mandated that the fairer sex should never cut their hair. Knowing that a severe beating was in Louie's immediate future, Mom tried to conceal my impromptu haircut. She busied herself with the task of rolling my hair in those ridiculous pink foam rollers. When Dad came home that evening, he was none the wiser and even commented on his little princess and her pink head. We left those rollers in all evening, and I even went to bed with them that night.

In the morning, Dad left for work before we got up, so he still had no idea about my new haircut. When we did take the rollers out, my hair had been transformed into the biggest afro imaginable. I looked like a six-year-old Foxy Cleopatra from the *Austin Powers* movie. I distinctly remember walking to the school bus that morning while trying to flatten my hair with my hands, nervous about being laughed at by my classmates.

Life went on as our normal. Mom and Dad fought, and Louie and I just tried to stay out of the way and keep Eric from creating too much chaos. Nothing noteworthy occurred until Christmas Eve 1979.

To kids, the longest season each year is the time between Thanksgiving and Christmas. The annual hype and frenzy wreak havoc on little ones who all but buzz with excitement and anticipation. Retailers do their best to showcase their newest and most coveted toys. Television commercials show kids whose lives are infinitely better now because they have said toy. School teachers make sure that classroom time is carved out for festive activity pages full of coloring, puzzles, and writing wish-lists for everything that is desired to be under the tree and in stockings on that most special morning. Street corners and shopping malls have stand-in Santas who pose for pictures while the real guy is wrapping up loose ends at the North Pole. Christmas carols permeate the air in stores, and sweet treats reserved especially for the season are abundant. Signs of Christmas can be found everywhere.

After much anticipation in our house that year, the season was drawing to an end and the night before Christmas was upon us. Strategizing our plan of attack for the next morning, Louie and I sat in the living room looking with excitement at the colorfully wrapped presents. Our tree was decorated with all the trappings of Christmas: ornaments, twinkling lights, candy canes, and each branch was dripping with the requisite spaghetti-thin silver icicles. Prominently displayed at the front of the tree were the special ornaments Louie and I had created at school—copious amounts of glitter sparkled as a beacon to Santa and Rudolph.

Christmas joy had overwhelmed our senses, which afforded us the luxury of drowning out the familiar sounds of Mom and Dad arguing in their bedroom. Suddenly the alarming sound of crashing glass and screaming voices jolted us out of our festive happiness and chased away the sugar plums that were dancing in our heads. I instinctively ran down the hall toward the commotion and saw Mom in the hallway, swinging her arms and striking Dad's head with her closed fists. Mom had a couple inches on Dad, and she had a solid, stocky, big-boned structure. She fought like a man, and I was afraid she was hurting him. This fight erupted because he had found her secret stash of liquor that she kept hidden under the photo albums and false bottom of her cedar hope chest. I guess "hope chest" meant she hoped that she wouldn't get caught with alcohol again.

Dad had a large glass bottle in his hand, and with all his might, he slammed it into the bathtub. CRASH! Shards of glass flew through the air as amber-colored alcohol splashed out of the tub. Then he turned and grabbed another bottle. CRASH! It exploded into a million pieces.

"Stop it!" I screamed, but they did not stop. "Stop it! Stop!" Even though I was screaming as loud as possible, they just didn't hear me over their fury. I'm sure Mom and Dad would have stopped their fighting if they'd known I was there, trying so hard to keep the peace. They were probably so far into their own heads and feelings that all they saw was red, all they heard was the force of their own blood pumping, all they tasted was the bitterness of adrenaline. I know, because this is what I experience when my emotions are running at fever pitch.

I then thought to myself that if I could just get in front of them, they would see me and have to stop. My vision, both eyesight and purpose, narrowed. Nothing else mattered to me—not Christmas, not Louie and Eric, not even my own safety. I ran into the bathroom, and just as Dad started to smash another bottle, he turned and saw me. I shrieked at the top of my lungs, "Stop fighting!" Dad put down the bottle he had cocked over his head, ready to throw, and he quickly scooped me up and ran me to the kitchen sink. I had no idea that I had stepped on a piece of glass and was bleeding. He sat me on the kitchen counter and held my leg still as the cool water cascaded over my bleeding wound. As he was wrapping my foot in a towel, we heard the front door slam shut. Mom took the opportunity to make her great escape.

Escape. Were we nothing more than captors, holding Mom

against her will? Was she so much of a free spirit that she just couldn't bear to be committed to a family? Did she only marry Dad and have babies because that's what was expected? These questions would continue to haunt me, especially later when I started my own family. The ugly truth was that Mom left us.

The next morning, Mom was not there and our excitement about opening Christmas presents was gone. Just like the remnants of bottles that lay in the bathtub, Christmas was shattered, our family was shattered, and more of my innocence was shattered. Even worse, guilt consumed me as I felt like it was my fault for interfering. I couldn't help but think that if I had only stayed in the living room with Louie and not tried to get them to stop fighting, they would have had their fight and the whole thing would have blown over. We could have had our Christmas and everything would have been "normal." I had no idea how close to the edge she really was. Even at six years of age, I knew our family wasn't perfect, but it was all I had. Now I had ruined it.

Dad in Japan, 1978

*Mom and Gayle
(around three or four months old)*

Eric, 1978

*Louie, 1st grade,
1978*

Me, 1978

Me, 1978

Louie, 1978

The Babysitter

With Mom gone and Dad still on active duty, he had to find reliable childcare for us. The wife of one of Dad's military buddies who also lived on base agreed to watch us. The addition of four more kids to their family of four certainly added a layer of complexity to their lives, but they welcomed us with open arms.

Miss Sharon was slender and on the tall side. She wore her hair in an afro and sometimes she wore a bandana head scarf. I don't remember her being fancy; but then again, who dresses up to watch kids? We'd go to their house after school, and when Dad had to travel, we would stay with them overnight.

Contrary to the era of his upbringing, Dad was not a prejudiced man and had friends of all races; his philosophy was that skin color didn't matter. In the war fields and swamps of Vietnam, all American soldiers were brothers. He carried this ethos back from the war and instilled it in his children in a time when racial equality, for much of the country, was still in its infancy.

I really didn't mind staying with Miss Sharon and her family. I actually liked the opportunity to see their model of a normal family dynamic. Miss Sharon and her husband worked in partnership with each other to raise their kids and run the house. Their efforts complemented each other and didn't undermine or undercut. It was here that I was exposed to a different kind of family. I learned that harmonious and nurturing family life wasn't a fairy tale. I often wonder what happened to Miss Sharon. I would love to locate her; it would be nice to reconnect with her after all these years.

Miss Sharon exposed us to a whole new culture of music, dance, and food. She was the first of many who shared with us a different way to experience life. We were treated to a new style of music with a driving beat. One such song was "Rapper's Delight." Louie and I would sing it until we had all the words memorized. This was the coolest song we had ever heard. With such an infectious tempo, we just couldn't be still. Miss Sharon taught us her dance moves, which were different from anything we had ever seen before. It was so fun to dance like she did.

Unfortunately, I didn't adapt to soul food as easily. Dinnertime was sometimes problematic, as food like frog legs, pickled pigs' feet, and a whole baked fish—eyes and all—would end up on our plates. I was convinced that she was trying to torture us. Who feeds this kind of food to kids? What was wrong with a good old-fashioned hamburger, macaroni and cheese, or pizza? Unwilling to lose this battle of the wills, I would cross my arms in sheer defiance and refuse to eat these ghastly concoctions. Her steadfast rule was that we couldn't leave the dinner table until we cleaned our plates. The stubborn streak that has served me well over the years also meant I ended up sleeping at that table many times.

Being obstinate cost me more than a good night's sleep in bed. Like birthdays and Christmas, some other things come around just once per year, and we were about to be treated to the annual viewing of *The Wizard of Oz*. I had been looking forward to this since I learned it was on the TV schedule. The Wicked Witch of the West was my favorite character—she had tons of personality and character flaws galore. I also loved to sing along with Dorothy, the Cowardly Lion, the Tin Man, and the Scarecrow as they merrily skipped down the yellow brick road, seeking the Wizard of Oz in the Emerald City.

I don't remember what was for dinner that night, but whatever it was I refused to eat it, even knowing full well that I would be denied the privilege of watching *The Wizard of Oz*. I cried and stomped my feet as Miss Sharon enforced her clean plate rule, but my antics did not change her mind. I learned that temper tantrums got me nowhere. Even though we didn't see eye to eye regarding mealtime, Miss Sharon was a delight and helped broaden our knowledge and culture. It was sad when we had to leave her. I love reflecting on my time with Miss Sharon because of the important connections we made together. She was the first person I spent meaningful time with who didn't look like me. She took us in without prejudice—not that I even knew what that meant—and she treated us like her own.

Unwittingly, she helped me define my sense of self and further develop my tenacity. I credit Miss Sharon for the life experiences she exposed me to, which also encouraged my natural curiosity to try new things throughout my life.

Goodbye...Hello

As Dad's duties increased exponentially, both with the Marines and at home since Mom left, he easily became overwhelmed. Louie, Eric, Gayle, and I were being shuffled back and forth between home and Miss Sharon more frequently. Dad felt like it was time to add some stability to our lives, and so he made arrangements for us to live with his parents. We packed up and headed back to Ohio.

We had traveled this route a few times before when we drove to Ohio to visit our grandparents. I always looked forward to a certain detour in the Smoky Mountains. Stopping at the same restaurant, The Pancake House, became our tradition. There we would be treated to hot and fluffy pancakes. Large picture windows afforded us spectacular panoramic views as the clouds hung low over the Great Smoky Mountains.

We arrived in Lebanon, Ohio, maybe ten minutes from

my humble beginnings in Waynesville. Dad got us settled with our grandparents and, as if he realized he'd left the oven on back in North Carolina, was on his way again. Had I known this was goodbye for more than a simple weekend visit, I would have savored one last long hug with Dad and probably been more melodramatic when he left shortly after getting us there.

Grandma and Grandpa were not wealthy, but they made do by converting the second story and basement of their mint-green home into apartments that they rented out to subsidize Grandpa's income. Their youngest son, Ivan, who was fourteen and the only remaining son still at home, enjoyed the autonomy of living in the top of the barn that he tricked out to convey his teen panache. With no other bedrooms to spare, Gayle and I slept on the living room floor while Louie and Eric slept on the floor of a different room.

Having both come from extremely large families, Grandma and Grandpa were used to making room to accommodate additional people. Between the two of them, they had twenty-nine siblings. Music and faith were the common threads that wove these two families together. Whenever family was gathered, they would assemble a spontaneous band and just start making music to simply praise the Lord and celebrate life. It wasn't unusual to hear banjos, fiddles, et cetera accompanied by cicadas and crickets on a warm summer night.

Their faith mandated modesty, which was evidenced by their personal appearance, especially the women, who were forbidden from cutting their hair or wearing pants or makeup. Moreover, the truly anointed have the gift of the Holy Spirit, which allows them to speak in tongues.

One time, I saw Grandma brushing her hair before going to bed. I knew her hair was long, but I didn't know it was past her knees. Hair that long was beyond my six-year-old comprehension. During the day, she would keep it rolled up and wrapped around her head, then she would pin it and cover it with a hair net, thus concealing one aspect of her covenant with God. Grandma took modesty to the nth degree when it came to her wardrobe. No matter the season, she would wear panty hose and a long woolen skirt with a blouse, vest, and sweater. She completed her ensemble with a pair of horn-rimmed glasses. But Grandma's faith didn't end there; that was just the beginning. She joyfully practiced what she preached by embodying the grace of the Holy Spirit.

Not belonging to any one church, Grandma would attend whichever service any of her brothers or sisters in faith were attending that day. Pentecostal churches are abundant in rural Ohio. Like ducklings following their mother, Louie, Eric, Gayle, and I would follow Grandma single file as she walked into the sacred space. We'd follow her down the center aisle and into an uncomfortable wooden pew.

Sitting shoulder to shoulder to shoulder, Grandma would cast a disapproving glance if our swinging legs would accidently kick the pew in front of us. Flipping through the hymnal was really the only other source of entertainment afforded to us, but most of the time Louie and I busied ourselves with the task of keeping Eric and Gayle hushed during scripture readings.

As soon as the music started, the Holy Spirit would fill Grandma. Her petite physique would jump up and run up and down the aisles waving her arms while speaking in a foreign language known only in heaven. Grandma was not fat, but she had soft curves that welcomed you home as she wrapped you in a bear hug. There she was, in God's glory, leading as others followed her around the church, singing and speaking in tongues. Louie and I were so embarrassed by this that we would sink down into the pews and snicker at the silliness of it all. Eric and Gayle were too young to understand the concept of self-consciousness. They just giggled and enjoyed the show.

Grandpa, not quite Grandma's polar opposite, was a judgmental man. His favorite phrase was "You better get right with the Lord." Grandma taught him to read using the bible, so this may have helped foster his austere philosophy on life. I fondly remember sitting in the living room at night, each of us, including Grandpa, taking turns reading the giant family bible.

Grandpa was a proud family man. His pet name for me was Doll Baby, and I loved that more than words could express. I got so very jealous when Grandpa began calling Gayle his Doll Baby.

Grandpa was well known in town. He was the former mayor of Corwin, Ohio, and he owned his own mechanic shop. Their backyard was always littered with broken-down cars awaiting his Midas touch. Grandpa's hands and nails were permanently stained, and he traded in the obligatory Old Spice grandpa scent for that of motor grease. In the spirit of the Christian way, if someone couldn't afford their car repair, he would happily do it for free. Make no mistake, he was a tough son of a gun. One time he was working under a car when the jack slipped and the rusty old jalopy he was working on came crashing down. The impact nearly tore his ear off, but he refused to go to the doctor. Instead, as if he were a light-year away from any other option, Grandpa grabbed the superglue and literally glued his ear back in place. And then, as if that wasn't secure enough, he wrapped some duct tape around his head and went back to work.

While we were getting to know our grandparents better, we had the added burden of fitting in at a new school. I don't remember if we started the school year in Lebanon or if we endured the discomfort of being the new kids who transferred in mid-semester. School was a relatively short walk for us, maybe a half mile, and Louie and I would walk there and back together. The novelty of walking to school was a welcome change from the bumpy ride of the crowded school bus on the base of Camp Lejeune.

I clearly remember the wonderful autumn in Ohio; the

colors of the season and the odor of skunks made quite an impression on me. Vibrant fall colors turned darker as leaves dried up and fell from the trees, nights grew longer, and there was an ever-increasing chill in the air—all signs of Halloween approaching. Louie, Eric, and I were enthusiastically waiting for The Night: the one night when kids get to assume a new persona, be it jovial or menacing. With this temporary identity they set out on a very important mission: to walk door to door and collect as much candy as possible, one piece at a time.

After negotiating with Grandma and Grandpa, we reached the agreement that if we could embark on this mission without them tagging along, which would only slow us down, we would promise to stay together…and behave ourselves.

As luck would have it, almost providentially, trick-or-treat night that year was unusually cold. While most kids were disappointed that they had to wear a coat over their carefully planned costumes, we were more than happy to do so because our coats *were* our costumes.

Louie, Eric, and I bundled up in our heavy winter coats and pulled our faux-fur-lined hoods over our heads. We raced to the front porch of house after house, each one of us straining to reach the doorbell before the others, then jockeying for a prime position in front of the door so we'd be first to get the loot. The cold night air was taking its toll, but we didn't mind. Rosy-cheeked, we'd wait patiently for someone to answer the door. "Trick or treat, smell my feet, give me something good to eat," we'd sing out in unison as if candy would be withheld until the recitation of such a demand.

Without fail, each homeowner would toss a piece or two of candy in our pillowcases. With puzzled looks on their faces, they would quiz us on our costumes. "We're Eskimos," we would gleefully explain as we rushed through our "thank you" and turned to head to the next house.

This Beggar's Night galvanized the bond that I shared with my siblings. Even something as simple as trick-or-treating, an activity that most kids take for granted, proved to each of us that we had each other through thick or thin. Yes, Mom may walk out on us. Sure, Dad may dump us off on his parents. We may not have the best of everything, but we'll always make the best of what we have.

Even though we gave up the luxuries of beds and bedrooms, we all liked being there with Grandma and Grandpa. Louie and Eric idolized Uncle Ivan and loved hearing about his latest conquest on the wrestling team at school. I was the little sister Uncle Ivan never had, and he rarely missed an opportunity to pick on me the way big brothers do. One time, Uncle Ivan claimed to have turned Louie into a frog, but I knew better and I let him know it by chanting "liar, liar, pants on fire." Then I searched all over for Louie, but I couldn't find him anywhere. Trying in vain to prove Uncle Ivan wrong, I was completely unaware that these two were in cahoots and I had walked right into their trap. Arms folded over his puffed-out chest, eyes half-closed, and lower jaw locked in defiance, Uncle Ivan shook his head from side to side, taunting me, saying that I'd never find Louie because he was now a frog.

Still unable to convince me, Uncle Ivan gave in and showed me the frog in his hands as proof of Louie's transmutation. With visible, tangible, and audible evidence, I immediately started to cry. Why would Uncle Ivan do such a horrible thing to Louie? We'd been through everything together, and he was my best friend! Now he's a FROG! Louie jumped out of hiding and they both laughed at me for believing their hoax.

Life went on as we settled into our new routines with Grandma, Grandpa, and Uncle Ivan. Grandma would hear this or that about someone in need, and she would immediately busy herself in prayer for them. Grandpa would repair cars with elbow grease and body parts with superglue and duct tape; because duct tape fixes everything. And Uncle Ivan would just be Uncle Ivan.

At bedtime, Grandpa imposed a "no talking after lights out" rule. Anyone who was found guilty of such a violation would find themselves on the business end of Grandpa's belt. Lying there in the dark, I would fixate on the fact that I was no longer Grandpa's Doll Baby and how Gayle, no more than eighteen months old, had taken that away from me. Jealousy consumed me, and I needed to act on that emotion. I would reach over and pull her hair. Her kinky red ringlets would straighten under the force of my pulling until the tension reached her scalp, and she would let out a cry. Soon after, I would hear Grandpa's heavy footsteps approaching, and I knew what would happen next. *HA! That serves her right for taking away my Doll Baby status*, I would think. I would soon come to deeply regret this jealousy and my actions.

I have vivid memories of a specific summer day at Grandma and Grandpa's house. We were playing outside in the summer sun and fresh air, working up a thirst that would soon be quenched by the cool water from the garden hose. Keeping a close eye on Uncle Ivan—I never quite trusted him after the incident when he claimed to have turned Louie into a frog—I was overjoyed to see that Dad had driven up from North Carolina. He was sitting on the back porch with Grandma and Grandpa and another couple that Dad introduced as his cousins. All I wanted to do was sit in Dad's lap and see him, talk with him, just simply *be* with him. It had been months since I had seen him, and since this visit was unannounced, I was reaching the peak of excitement. Dad kept nudging me off his lap and directing me to go play. So I did, but kids are smarter than they get credit for, and I could definitely tell something was going on.

While I was playing, I would steal glances in the direction of the adults. Their faces were serious, and they all spoke in hushed tones. None of this was typical for a spur-of-the-moment family reunion and I knew it. Before long, Dad announced that he was taking us back to North Carolina. He instructed us to pack up our belongings and get in the car. We hugged Grandma, Grandpa, and Uncle Ivan goodbye, and then we were on our way. As Dad's cream-colored El Camino pulled out of the driveway with me, Louie, and Eric all lined up on the bench-style front seat, I noticed one tiny little sibling was absent, and I frantically alerted Dad that we had mistakenly left Gayle behind. "DAD! We can't leave yet. We don't have Gayle!"

"No, that's okay," Dad replied. "We're going to get Gayle later."

"Oh, she gets to stay with Grandma and Grandpa?" I responded. My seven-year-old intellect justified this strategy as a simple matter of logistics. After all, there was no room for her in the front seat with us.

I began to miss Gayle immediately. My secret mantra became: "I take it back. I DON'T wish to be the only girl in the family."

The long drive down to North Carolina was miserable. I exiled myself to a dark place of guilt and bitter shame as I recalled all the times I resented Gayle's mere existence and underhandedly taunted her. Even at that tender age of seven, I inherently understood my role as the big sister. I should have been protecting her.

I couldn't have been more shocked when we finally reached our home in Camp Lejeune to find we had a stepmom!

Myra was just eighteen years old. She was slender and had a rich olive complexion, curly blond hair, and wore glasses. To add insult to injury, Myra had two daughters: April, who was four, and a baby who was about Gayle's age. This only confounded matters in my head. Why did we have to give up *our* baby sister? Clearly there was room in the family for a baby. I wanted Gayle back!

Needless to say, we were not the blended family after which *The Brady Bunch* was modeled. April was bratty and liked to hit me and pull my hair. Myra was blind to her daughter's malevolent behaviors but found creative ways to punish us for any infraction. Among her favorites were making us balance on one foot in the corner of the room with our hands in the air, making us jump up and down in the living room until she allowed us to stop, and washing our mouths out with a bar of soap—which burned in a special way that was counterintuitive; soap smells so nice but tastes awful. One time, Eric—only four years old—wet his pants, so she put him in a diaper and made him walk the neighborhood holding a sign that read "I pee my pants like a little baby."

I weathered the Myra storm as my rightful punishment for the treatment I gave Gayle. The life lesson I learned here is to be careful what you wish for, because you just might get it.

It wasn't a big secret that Dad and Myra weren't a match made in heaven. We would overhear their fights on a regular basis. Looking back, I can see that Dad married Myra to secure childcare—the missing link he needed in order to get us back from Ohio. But this plan backfired. During one of their fights I heard the ultimatum. Myra finally said what she had undoubtedly been thinking for a long time: "It's either your kids or me!"

"Coincidentally," Mom showed up to claim us kids not too long after this blowup. Clearly, Dad let his hormones and not his heart decide our fate. When Mom stepped out of the truck, she was not alone. She was accompanied by her new boyfriend, Stan, and a baby less than six months old. They arrived in a small brown truck with a white cab on the back. Stan was almost as tall as Mom; he was very tan and had brown hair and light blue eyes. He must have had a physical job because he was very trim and muscular.

Lined up in the front yard like stair steps, Louie, Eric, and I stood, each with a packed bag by our feet. Even before she uttered a word, Mom's expression said it all. I could tell she noticed Gayle's absence. "Where's Gayle?" The sharp edge in her voice conveyed her resentment over having to take us back, or seeing Dad again, or both. I was focused so intently on Mom that I didn't hear Dad's response. It didn't matter, though. I was painfully aware that Gayle was gone, given to a new family. I would probably never see her again. As if Mom had any right to stake a claim on the family she'd abandoned over a year before, she flew into a rage. "You motherfucker!"

Mom's pace quickened as she approached Dad. Immediately, I flashed back to that Christmas Eve fight when she'd left us. Before I could jump into action, and I most certainly would have, Stan, who was walking behind Mom, wrapped his arm around her middle and used all his strength to restrain her. He lifted her off the ground to prevent her from advancing farther toward Dad. Mom's arms were swinging like a windmill as she made every effort to land a few strikes on Dad. It would have been funny if it weren't so real. She looked just like a wild child who'd been raised by wolves and refused to adjust to the social mores of humans.

Stan rushed her back to the truck as he hollered at us to finish our goodbyes with our father and jump in the back. Panicking at the urgency of the situation, Louie, Eric, and I were unable to process what had just happened. Compliant to this stranger's command, we hugged Dad goodbye. He was crying and we were crying, but I found a sliver of hope in his promise that he would visit us soon. Acutely uncertain of our future, Louie, Eric, and I climbed into the truck and we sped away.

Stan navigated the streets of the base as we made our way out of Camp Lejeune. Peering out of the windows of the truck's topper, I watched as familiar sights grew more and more distant. Mom was seething about what had transpired, and she was even more irate about Dad giving Gayle away.

She slid open the window that separated the cab from the cargo bed where we were. Andy was in her arms. He was not being cradled like a baby; rather, she clung to him like a possession. "I'll be dammed if someone else is going to raise my kid. We'll get Gayle back. I guaran-*damn*-tee it!"

In that moment, I was all "Team Mom." She wasn't the prototypical fairy tale mom who kissed boo-boos and skinned knees, but she was my mom and, in that moment, I felt like she actually did care about us. She was on a mission to make us whole again.

But I quickly learned that Mom's campaign to find Gayle and regain custody was about as short-lived as a gnat's life cycle. Sure, in the heat of the moment, she fiercely advocated for Gayle's return, but once she calmed down, and especially as life's demands waged war on her, she realized that the four of us were more than she could handle. So much for the adage "the more the merrier." We never saw Gayle again.

I was slowly realizing that Mom's return to claim us was less about her maternal instinct or love for us and more about her hatred of Dad. It was as if she were keeping score (she probably was), and retrieving us was one more point for her.

In the span of twelve to sixteen months, Dad came home from war, we moved as a family to North Carolina, that failed and Mom left, and Dad sent us kids back to Ohio to live with Grandma and Grandpa. As soon as we felt comfortable, Dad reclaimed us and back to North Carolina we went. As abruptly as she left us, Mom returned to take us back. In the middle of all of this Gayle was born and was eventually surrendered to strangers. I didn't know at the time how our constantly changing living conditions closely paralleled the lives of kids in the foster care system. We bounced around like ping-pong balls, never truly knowing if we'd go to bed in the same place where we woke up on any given day.

Grandpa and Grandma
circa 1980

Gayle at two years old

Nelly

We drove nonstop from Camp Lejeune and settled in Secane, Pennsylvania, just twenty miles southwest of Philadelphia. Mom, Louie, Eric, Andy, and I lived above a bar named Stingers. Our tiny apartment was the size of a hotel room with one bed, a crib, and a bathroom. The adjoining room had only a bed and bathroom, and that's where Stan lived. Mom often slept in Stan's room, and the rest of us shared the bed in the other room. Mom bartended at Stingers, but I have no idea what Stan did. While Mom was working, she would leave Andy in a bassinet in the bar's ghost town of a dining room, and Eric would play on the floor at Mom's feet behind the bar. Louie and I needed much less supervision, so we were often left to our own devices.

Catty-corner from Stingers was Our Lady of Fatima convent. Louie and I would sometimes spend time in their yard playing cards, and when the sisters would return from the grocery store, we'd help them carry in groceries. I liked watching them walk in a single file line with their black habits. It made me think of a parade of penguins and put a smile on my face every time.

When we were not allowed to wander, Louie and I played in the dumpster behind Stingers. This was no ordinary dumpster. It was industrial size, the kind you'd find at a construction site, and when it was empty, it was a playhouse, a cave of wonders, and a terrific hiding place. When it was full, we would sift through the rubbish. You'd be surprised what treasures you can find in a dumpster. We once found a box of perfectly fine greeting cards.

On one particular day, I found the best treasure ever. She was a large cloth doll, almost as tall as I was. Her big blue eyes and pink lips were embroidered on her face, but her nose was a simple triangle that was drawn on. Her hair was yellow yarn with a braid on each side. There was a rip across the front of her neck that exposed fluffy pillow filling and made her head flop backward. She was filthy. She wore a bonnet on her head and a smock-style dress with dirty white ruffles at the wrists. She had little black ballerina slippers that were sewn on her feet.

This doll had been discarded because she was no longer perfect. I found myself wondering where she came from and what circumstances brought her to this rusty, graffiti-covered dumpster. I imagined that she was a long-anticipated gift—birthday or Christmas—for some special little girl. She was undoubtedly received with smiles, giggles, and cuddles from that little girl. Similarly, I was a long-anticipated gift, and I, too, had been received with smiles, giggles, and cuddles. I saw her rips, tears, and filth as visual evidence of mistreatment, abuse, and neglect. While my spirit's battle scars were invisible, but real all the same, the dumpster doll faced the world with all of her scars showing.

I named her Nelly because she reminded me of a character from *Little House on the Prairie*. I cleaned her up the best I could, and I played with her long hair until I taught myself how to braid it. It was in my DNA to care for Nelly, even though I never saw this sort of behavior modeled by Mom. It wasn't long before Nelly's flaws vanished, more figuratively than literally. To me she was perfect. Not of flesh and blood, but fabric and fluff, she became my new best friend. Aside from Louie, Nelly was my first best friend.

Sitting Nelly across from me, we would have imaginary tea parties. The best part about make-believe is that it can be as fancy as your wildest dreams. We, of course, "sipped" tea from the most exquisite teacups in the land. The peanuts and pretzels I smuggled out of Stingers became our crumpets and finger sandwiches, served on the rarest and most ornate china under the guise of paper plates and napkins for anyone who spied upon us. I was transfixed by the world of make-believe and reveled in the escape that it afforded me.

Nelly was there as I fell asleep and there when I woke. She came to school with me, and she was at my side when I ate. Nelly would even accompany me when I would play in the convent yard across the street. Nelly helped fill the void that was created when Gayle was given away.

Nelly was my confidante; she was the one who would patiently listen to all of my deepest, darkest secrets without judgment or disdain. With a serene smile on her face, Nelly absorbed my pain and soothed my fears. It was Nelly who bore the brunt of my outbursts when I would buckle under the pressure of being me.

Round Two

When Mom and Stan went out, our neighbor, Charles, would watch us. We actually enjoyed spending time in Charles' apartment. He had a TV and would let us watch it. Charles was always smiling and had a calm demeanor; he was generally regarded as the friendly neighbor man. Before long, Louie and Eric would get sleepy and Charles would send them back to our apartment for bed. But because I was still wide awake, I stayed with Charles to watch more TV. His soft tone put me at ease at a time when I was having nightmares and trouble sleeping because I missed Dad so much.

Lying in bed next to me while we were watching TV, Charles would slide his hand into my panties and fondle me; he claimed that it would help me sleep. This time, unlike my experience with Uncle Jeff, I liked the sensation this elicited, and worried about what that said about me. The juxtaposition of his large and callused hands violating my innocent virginity assaulted my sense of well-being—both physically and emotionally.

The comfort and pleasure associated with my physical reaction to his touch would wreak havoc with my psyche for years to come. I began to explore on my own and learned what I liked. The escape I found in this ecstasy transported me to a state of euphoria away from everything in my life that I hated. My new addiction was always just under the surface, waiting for otherwise benign triggers that lay hidden like an abandoned minefield. I was susceptible to shame and self-loathing, believing that I was a sexual deviant.

Not long after, we moved to an apartment above a lumber yard in Horsham, Pennsylvania. All four of us kids shared a bedroom, and Mom and Stan had the other bedroom. Louie and I used to walk across a four-lane highway to get to the nearby convenience store to buy penny candies, or sometimes Mom would send us for staples like milk and bread. Often our empty tummies demanded food so we would steal fruit pie snacks. We were in there so frequently that the employees knew us by name and where we lived; or at least they knew the general direction we came from.

Mom wasn't any happier with Stan than she was with Dad. They had frequent fights, usually fueled by alcohol. We became accustomed to these arguments, which regularly evolved into very physical fights: loud screaming, pushing, shoving, and punching. Both of them would actively and equally participate in these knock-down, drag-out fights. Louie or I would sometimes jump on Stan's back when we thought he was being too rough with Mom, only to get thrown to the floor or yelled at to go to our room.

My hopeful "Team Mom" attitude had waned to the point of nonexistence by now. It was abundantly clear that she would never change. And Stan clearly wasn't cut out for family life either. I used to wish that Stan would just go away and leave with Mom.

We tried to patiently endure all of Mom and Stan's antics, which ranged from mild disagreements to full-fledged fights. We were never lucky enough for them to use the silent treatment on each other.

One time, yet another fight broke out in the middle of the night. Their loud voices pierced the silence that accompanies the hours after midnight. We heard so much ruckus and unrest that Louie and I peeked out of our bedroom to see Mom and Stan in a violent fight. Having seen and heard enough, Louie fled the scene, but in the chaos I didn't even notice that he'd left. Their rage carried them out of the apartment and into the hall. It was so fierce that Stan managed to knock Mom unconscious. I remember seeing Mom lying on the hallway floor outside of the apartment. I could not wake her, so I called out for Louie to come and help me.

Louie didn't respond to my appeals and I couldn't find him anywhere. I looked in both bedrooms and the bathroom.

No Louie. I grabbed my coat and looked outside. I walked all around the building, looking under and behind the bushes, in the adjacent lumber yard, and even in the dumpster. Still no Louie. There was only one place left that I could think of where he would be, so I sprinted across the four-lane highway and headed to the 7-Eleven. Sure enough, there he was, asleep in the corner behind the pinball machine, crouched in the corner in his pajamas and winter coat, soaking wet with urine.

When the chips are down and the world is against you, when all you want is to feel safe and see a friendly face, you go home to familiarity, to comfort, to where you get fed—literally and figuratively. My older brother sought refuge in a convenience store rather than in his own home. Why? Because this was where people smiled when they saw him; they didn't see him as a burden or another mouth to feed. This was where he played video games with quarters he found. This was where people treated him like a kid—they didn't bark commands and expect him to deal with life on terms beyond his years.

By the time I was able to wake Louie and convince him to return home, Mom had regained consciousness and dragged herself to bed. I was struck by the fact that she probably didn't even realize we were missing.

Guardian Angels

The lack of parental supervision was unbelievable, yet undeniable, and the neglect was atrocious. But the worst thing that happened to me was quite physical and almost cost me my life.

On December 8, 1981, while crossing the highway to get to the 7-Eleven, as I had done many times, I was hit by a drunk driver who immediately sped away. I can only imagine the scene as one of intense gore and tragedy. An eight-year-old is no match for a speeding car. I undoubtedly became airborne as I bounced off the car's bumper.

In the era before mobile phones and access to the world at our fingertips, witnesses would have needed to pull off the highway and find a pay phone so they could call for help. The nearby 7-Eleven was surely where they went. Natural and morbid curiosity drew onlookers to my side. The employees at the store recognized me and told the first responders where I lived.

Trying to avoid bringing a Jane Doe to the hospital, police attempted to locate my home and parents while EMS triaged and stabilized me. Once they located Mom, the police escorted her, with Louie in tow, to the ambulance so she could identify me. As they opened the back of the ambulance, Louie's account of Mom's reaction was one akin to the revulsion of smelling a foul odor. Louie said he knew it was me immediately by the sight of my coat, which was left ragged and bloodied.

My medical records revealed that I was in shock and had to be intubated and placed on a respirator. I was resuscitated in the emergency room and ended up in a coma for three days. I had multiple head and scalp lacerations along with gashes on my wrist and legs. I was covered with road rash where my clothes shredded from the impact of landing and skidding on the pavement. I was diagnosed with right sixth nerve palsy, which left me cross-eyed. Mercifully, I had amnesia and couldn't remember the horrific event. I was rushed into exploratory surgery which revealed that I had a shattered kidney that had to be removed, a shattered pelvis, fractured ribs, and a lacerated liver and bowels. All of this damage was surgically corrected.

Movies get it right when they portray coma victims waking slowly under a cloud of confusion. Only Disney can get away with the *Sleeping Beauty* story line where the princess awakens bright-eyed and cheerful from a single kiss.

As I awoke, I slowly became aware of my surroundings: the strange bed with side rails, the IV drip that was hanging above me. I followed the slender tubing with my eyes until its end plunged deep into the back of my hand where medical tape secured the line. My vision was blurred and obstructed by the swelling in my face. Beeping monitors gauged my heart rate and blood pressure. Nurses and aides came to my ICU room on a regular basis. "How are we feeling today?" they would ask as they noted my vitals, replaced IV drips, emptied my catheter bag, or changed my wound dressings.

I was in shock the first time I looked in the mirror; I didn't even recognize myself. I looked like Frankenstein with broken parts pieced together with large ugly stitches. I had stitches in my head, face, arm, and torso. I was swollen, bruised, abraded, scabbed, and half of my head was shaved. It's funny how personal identity isn't something you think about—especially as a kid—until it's altered. I looked in the mirror but didn't see me. Who was I now, some sad hospital kid?

Notes from the staff psychiatrist documented my depressed affect and that I tried to conceal it. They also expressed concern for the lack of parental presence and involvement in my recovery. Even though the school district offered childcare arrangements so Mom could be with me, she never came.

I grew accustomed to the steady traffic flow of doctors, nurses, nurses' aides, and volunteers. I knew them all by sight, and even started remembering their names.

One day, having just returned from x-ray, a nurse's aide

was helping me settle back in bed when some guy walked in. He wasn't dressed like a doctor, and his face showed more concern than the business-as-usual nurses who tended to me. He didn't reach for my chart to review medical notes. He glanced at the monitors that surrounded me, but not to get data pertaining to my status. Rather, he looked unsettled by their presence. I didn't recognize him, but he acted like he knew me. As he stepped closer to hand me a teddy bear, I saw tears welling in his eyes. His chin quivered and he bit his lip. Then he whispered, "I…I love you." My amnesia prevented me from recognizing him. This man's heart broke even more when I stared blankly at him as he strained to get words out. "It's me, hun. It's Dad." As soon as he heard about the accident he came to visit me, but had to immediately return to North Carolina.

Once I was stable, I was moved from the ICU into a regular hospital room. Since I was being weaned off of heavy sedation, I was able to notice more of my surroundings—the sterile white tile on the walls and shiny linoleum floor. There was a curtain that was suspended from a track on the ceiling. This is what allowed my room to be called semi-private, but I could still hear the rhythmic beeping of my octogenarian roommate's monitors.

The world immediately outside my hospital room—the hallway and nearby nurse's station—offered an array of additional sights and sounds. For example, the cadence of the wheels on the food cart three times each day, which I could hear draw near and then fade away again as the aides made their way down the hall delivering meals to each patient. Hospital food is the butt of every hospital joke, and I certainly can commiserate. The only thing I ever enjoyed came in the form of translucent jiggly cubes. It could be slurped or chewed, and it was cool and soothing to my persistent dry mouth. And then there was the constant intercom paging. In the days before cell phones or even pagers, doctors were beckoned via intercom. The nurse's station offered a cacophony of beeps and alarms that corresponded to each bed in every room.

While in the hospital, I was well known as the kid without: without any toys to play with, without the benefit of family visits, without the ability to get out of bed. There I was in room 211, half bald, cross-eyed, stitches everywhere, with a roommate. I looked like my tattered, filthy rag doll, Nelly. As Christmas approached, I could feel the depression, which I was trying to suppress, begin to tighten its grip. Sure, the hospital was decorated, but a hospital is still a hospital.

I started receiving toys from well-wishers. I suspect they came from hospital staff, teachers from school, and anonymous donors. Stuffed animals—some bigger than me—Barbie dolls, baby dolls, anything a little girl could possibly want. Each doll or toy delivery was accompanied by much fanfare from a nurse or candy stripe volunteer. They would cheerfully announce that a new visitor was coming to see me. This stash of toys grew so rapidly that the nurses half-jokingly told my roommate that she might need to move to a new room to allow space for all my "visitors."

One day, I received a phone call. It was the entire student body of Pennypack Elementary. They were gathered in the gymnasium for the annual Christmas assembly, and they called to sing Christmas carols just for me. I could visualize all the children congregated and seated Indian-style on the gym floor, and I could hear the reverberation off the gymnasium walls. All of these acts went a long way to help restore my faith in humanity and see the beauty through the ugliness that surrounded me.

According to the medical notes, the hospital staff was my primary source of support and companionship. The main nurse charged with my care was Faye. She was a petite woman with red hair and a neat accent. "Good morning, ma dear. How arh you today?" She sounded like she was from Boston. Faye was beautiful inside and out, and she had a smile that could light up any room, even a hospital room. She made me feel loved, and special, and beautiful, and I liked her instantly. We spent lots of one-on-one time together, and she dedicated herself to getting me through the healing process.

When it came time to use the bedpan, I resisted and pouted. I hated that thing. It was cold and awkward, not to mention the tiny remaining bit of modesty that is surrendered when someone has to help you use it. So I asked Faye if she could help me get to the bathroom. With all my injuries, especially a broken pelvic bone, walking to the toilet was next to impossible, but Faye never gave up on me. She worked with me daily as I relearned how to walk. There I was, God-awful hospital gown hanging on me, and any otherwise exposed skin covered in bruises, sutures, and bandages. I grasped the hand grips of the pediatric-sized walker so tightly that my knuckles were white. Each step, excruciating; each step, Faye. She stayed by my side, rolling along on her little stool on wheels. She never let me go, and I never felt so safe. Fierce determination propelled me, and little by little, I continued to make progress, walking farther each day. Faye would increase her distance from me until I was able to make it to the bathroom. As if I were the only patient she cared for, Faye would stay nearby as I worked my way up and down the halls of the hospital. The cheers and encouragement from the staff only fueled my heart's determination to get better and impress them.

My recovery was bittersweet, as I knew getting better meant leaving the comfort and safety of this place and these wonderful people. I spent nearly four weeks in Warminster General Hospital, and the staff there were nicer to me than anyone in my family. As I started to heal, my thoughts turned to my brothers, and I began to worry about them stuck at home without the benefit of the regular, wholesome meals that I was receiving.

Faye was keenly aware of my mounting medical bills and recognized our need for legal representation. She put Mom in touch with her fiancé, who was an attorney. Of course, Mom quickly contacted the attorney, thinking she could sue the drunk driver or his insurance company and get a big payday.

Alan Williams became my attorney and worked tirelessly to protect my interest. Seeing through Mom's façade, he was the catalyst for a new life for me. Occasionally Mom would "borrow" money from Mr. Williams under the guise of caring for us kids, but instead she used that money for drugs. I thank the Lord that by the time the court case was settled, I was a ward of the state and Mr. Williams had invested my settlement in an annuity not to be touched until I became an adult. Looking back, it was a blessing in disguise.

I am so grateful for those who intervened to save my life, restore my health, and protect my future. I often reflect on this experience and try to remember, as we move through our busy lives, that we need to remain vigilant because we never know when we'll be given the opportunity to become someone's guardian angel.

Alan Williams and Faye circa 1985

A New Normal

Eventually, things began to turn around. I was released from the hospital the day after Christmas. My recovery was on track with the help of a home nurse, and the school district provided a tutor so I could catch up with my class. Mom even made an effort to get me back to the hospital for a follow-up appointment. I remember we had to hitchhike four miles in the dead of winter to the hospital that day. I was still in a tremendous amount of pain. Looking back, it seems that Mom was trying to put on a good show for any would-be child advocates. Little good that did, because in the privacy of our home, she reverted to her old ways of abuse and neglect.

Sometimes Mom and Stan would invite their friends over from the bar. This couple had two kids: a son Louie's age and a daughter who was my age. We occupied ourselves while the adults played cards, smoked, drank, and laughed. Andy was only eight or nine months old, so he didn't need a playmate, but there was no one for five-year-old Eric to play with. We teased Eric to keep him from wanting to play with us. He was so hyperactive, it was like giving an energy drink to the Tasmanian Devil. I remember Mom offering him a drink of Jack Daniel's straight from the bottle. I watched through the haze of cigarette smoke that filled the room. It was a train wreck. I was horrified that she was giving him alcohol, but I couldn't look away. Without even considering that she might give him anything but Kool-Aid or Coke, Eric snatched the liquor bottle from her hand that still had a cigarette wedged between her first two fingers and took a gulp. Curious horror kept me locked in on the scene that was unfolding. Eric's head jolted back and then to the left and right as he tried to escape the bitter burn of the alcohol. Poor little Eric contorted his face, reacting to the assault on his innocent taste buds the way babies do when they taste lemons for the first time.

This was hilarious to Mom and her guests. The very instant the alcohol touched his tongue, Eric's pain was evident, but he had already swallowed and the burn streamed to the back of his mouth and down his throat. In that moment, I focused so intently on Eric. I tried to will myself into his being and absorb his suffering. Once Eric recovered, he proceeded to interrupt the card game. Mom then mixed a cocktail of Coke with a few splashes of Jack Daniel's, poured it in one of Andy's baby bottles, handed it to Eric, and sent him off to bed. It wasn't long before Eric was down for the count.

One day, out of the blue, not too long after my release from the hospital, Mom and Stan packed us all up in a car and we drove to upstate New York to visit Mom's mom, Frances. I remember being in pain and nauseated during the car ride. Thankfully, I was able to sleep during much of the trip. This time is foggy, as I have only sketchy memories of how we got to New York. We didn't own a car, so it's highly probable that Stan borrowed one for this trip. I don't recall a particularly warm welcome when we met our grandmother for the first time, so I am left to believe that she considered us nothing more than mere background noise to our mother's miserable existence. Stan didn't stay with us during this visit. He must have driven back to Pennsylvania to return the car he borrowed.

We left New York as abruptly as we arrived, but this time Mom summoned us from sleep in the middle of the night. Her hand nudging my shoulder, she woke me from my light slumber. Because I was still recovering from my accident, I was allowed to sleep on the couch when everyone else made do on the floor. I was bleary-eyed and confused, but I followed Louie's lead. We all piled silently in Frances' car without so much as a goodbye to our estranged grandmother.

Looking back, it seems that the whole reason for this brief mother/daughter reunion was so Mom could steal her money and car. It is my belief that Mom was evading the pending scrutiny of the local child welfare agency that was undoubtedly notified by the hospital, or perhaps we were skipping town to avoid eviction.

As soon as we returned to our home in Pennsylvania, Mom directed us to fill trash bags with our clothes and take them to the car. The urgency in her voice foretold of a pending yet unknown scenario that we needed to escape. As if the apartment were on fire, we had only moments to flee. I was distraught when I was forbidden from bringing any of my new toys. I even had to leave Nelly behind. As stealthily as ninjas, we climbed into the car with our trash bags of clothes and drove away. A new adventure was afoot.

That car was not only our transportation, it was our temporary home as well. I recall nesting with my brothers on the lumpy bags of clothes that became our bed. We also used clothes as makeshift blankets and pillows.

On more than one occasion, I stirred awake in the dark of night when the rhythm of the road stopped. Through hazy, sleepy eyes, I'd notice we were parked—with the car running—along the perimeter of a gas station or convenience store property. Sometimes we were simply sitting idle on the highway's shoulder. I could feel the force of eighteen-wheelers as they barreled down the highway past our parked car. In the front seat, Mom would be sitting behind the wheel. Although she could drive, Stan did most of it. Within a minute or so I would see Stan running toward us. He would hop in the car and we would speed away.

Sometimes on this trip we would make an overnight stop at the homes of Stan's friends or family. This was our only opportunity to bathe and maybe eat a meal that wasn't in a paper bag and passed through the car window. After weeks of driving, eventually the car broke down on the side of the highway. Whatever was wrong with it, Stan couldn't just MacGyver a repair. Fortunately, Stan located a cousin who was close enough to come to our rescue. This cousin came and picked us up from the side of the highway and arranged to have our car towed back to his place. We all stayed there while Stan and his cousin worked on the car.

Finally, we'd made it to easy street, I thought. This family must be rich; they had a color TV and an Atari system. Such luxuries were reserved for society's elite. Louie and I tried to perfect our Pac-Man and Centipede skills, games we hadn't played since our days at the 7-Eleven, which felt like a hundred years ago. Alas! The car was road-worthy and we were on the road again, leaving all the trappings of the privileged behind.

Three months passed as we meandered our way south. We finally stopped at what Mom and Stan deemed an acceptable residence in Florida. Our first permanent residence as Floridians was an old rusted-out trailer that was parked in the middle of a barren plot of land surrounded by an orange grove. On the far end of the area, about a football-field length away, sat two more trailers. What separated us from those two distant trailers was an expanse of sand. Under the midsummer Florida sun without any discernible shade, this sand became blistering hot and therefore an ominous barrier that was nearly as effective as an eight-foot barbed wire fence. Nearly.

Louie and I would compete to see who could stand barefoot the longest on the scorching sand. Five seconds was the best either of us could tolerate on the tender soles of our feet. In order to traverse the sand without sizzling our feet, Louie and I would fill Big Gulp cups with water and douse the sand to cool it before stepping. Step by intrepid step, we made our way across. The sweet reward for braving our personal lava field was found in the refuge of the trailers' occupants across the way.

In all, there were about twenty Latinos. It appeared to be a single family; the revered wise elders who had earned their place as overseers of the family, the next generation who were the hardworking parents and caregivers, and then all the children who ranged from nursing infants to adolescents. None of them spoke English, and we spoke no Spanish.

Reminiscent of the prodigal son, this family immediately welcomed us with warm smiles and open arms. We gained instant playmates in the children, and wholesome nutrition from the adults as we feasted on homemade tamales and tortillas. This surrogate parental compassion surpassed any language barrier. Moreover, in the purest Christian sense, these kind and generous people freely and joyfully shared what little they had.

I had no reason to dislike or distrust these people. In fact, I believe my life experiences, even at this tender age, afforded me the opportunity to look past superficial attributes like skin color or nationality and peer into people's hearts and souls. It's their character, their moral fiber, that attracts me, not their bank account or any other tangible possession. This experience served to reinforce my already well-established belief.

When we weren't baby sitting Eric and Andy or playing with our newly acquired friends, Louie and I sometimes occupied ourselves by collecting discarded glass bottles from along the side of the road. We must have been some kind of sight as we walked along the gravel shoulder of the two-lane highway. It wasn't a particularly busy stretch of road; maybe ten cars and trucks passed us in a fifteen-minute span. We found all sorts of debris, organic and man-made, too many cigarette butts to count and lots of broken glass. But the worst was the gruesome evidence of speeding cars and trucks disturbing the circle of life. The abundance of flattened opossums, birds, turtles, and more roadkill made me queasy, especially the stench of decay and the swarms of flies that feasted on these dreadful carcasses.

To pass the time and keep ourselves entertained, we cheerfully belted out our favorite songs. "Chicken in a bread pan pickin' out dough. Granny does your dog bite? No, child, no." I would dance a little jig while Louie sang the fiddle riff of "The Devil Went Down to Georgia." We'd giggle as I accidentally kicked off my flip-flop when I kicked too high. On one foot and arms out at my sides, I'd hop a few feet down the road to reclaim my wayward footwear. Songs from the Beach Boys, John Cougar Mellencamp, and one of my Christmas favorites, "Grandma Got Run Over by a Reindeer," were also part of our repertoire. We were hot and sweaty, sunburned, and so very thirsty, but these are among some of my fondest childhood memories spent with my big brother.

Once we had accumulated as many bottles as we could carry in our arms, we walked several miles to the store to cash them in at ten cents each. Payday! We stretched our money as far as we could by buying from the penny candy bins. We also used our hard-earned fortune to buy other luxuries such as soda. Mr. Pibb was our favorite.

Our shopping spree ended as we emerged from the store with a brown paper bag containing our budget candy preferences: Mary Janes and Bit-o-Honey, and we splurged on the five-cent Blow Pops and fifteen-cent Jolly Ranchers. Louie and I made sure to buy enough candy to share with Eric and the nearby Latino children, and we always managed to get something that Andy could have, too. We cherished this time as it was a desperately needed respite from our home life.

All signs pointed to our newly established stability. We moved out of the trailer and into a rented house. This house had a TV and three bedrooms, which meant that Louie and I shared one, Eric and Andy shared one, and the other bedroom was for Mom and Stan. Ranch style and hunter green, our new house was complete with junk accumulated in the yard. You could find anything from old household appliances to a large bathtub sitting on paver stones. With a little resourcefulness and an old towel to plug the drain, Louie and I converted that bathtub into a makeshift pool. We'd fill the tub with water and jump in to escape the steamy Florida heat.

Given the heat index during Florida's summers, it should be illegal to build a home and exclude air conditioning. Our rented ranch home was a sweat box. As the mercury climbed, our relief came in the form of box fans that we placed in open windows and doorways. The working theory was that the fans would draw in the outside air and help circulate it throughout the house. But the only things that circulated were flies. Mom hated having flies in the house, so she would hang a multitude of tacky fly strips from the ceiling to capture the pests. As effective as these icky yellow sticky strips were at catching flies, they were also quite effective at catching me. As I would run through the house playing tag or hide-and-seek with Louie and Eric, I would frequently get caught by these gross strips. My gleeful play would be interrupted by the harsh jolt of a wisp or handful of hair, unexpectedly coated in adhesive goo and the dead and dying flies it captured. It was impossible to free myself from the seventh circle of fly-hell without being cut free. The result was chopped hair that publicized my failure to steer clear of these booby traps. The strips themselves taunted me with yellow sticky gunk, fly carcasses, and now, my own hair.

By this time, Eric was a little older and still trying Mom's nerves, so Louie and I were supposed to take him with us when we went out to play. Across from the house was a golf course. A strategically planted treeline offered privacy and seclusion for the golfers, but that didn't stop us. Splashing and giggling, Louie and I would swim freely in the water-hazard pond. Why not? It was a wonderful step up from our makeshift bathtub-pool.

Golf balls were the new glass bottles. Our entrepreneur spirits kicked in when we discovered that we could recover sunken golf balls from the water hazard and cash them in for money in the pro shop. It was a win/win proposition; the golf course got their balls back, while we got to cool off in the water and cash in on our efforts.

One day, the whole family went over to the pond at the golf course for a swim. Mom was deathly afraid of the water and never learned to swim. She was planning on sitting out with Andy while I splashed in the water with Louie and Eric. Stan started to tease Mom and pull her toward the water's edge. Knowing from experience that anything physical between the two of them had the volatile potential to end badly, the boys and I got out of the water.

Eventually, Stan gave up on getting Mom in the water and announced that it was time for sixteen-month-old Andy to learn to swim. Stan picked Andy up and walked over to the water's edge. With Andy in his arms, he bent at the waist and swung Andy back and forth. Then, on the upswing, Andy went airborne. To everyone's horror, Stan threw him in the water. I watched, frozen, as my baby brother sailed through the air and splashed down in the center of the pond. Like an anvil, Andy immediately sunk to the bottom of the three-foot pond. Mom was enraged and began to scream, "Get my fucking baby out of the fucking water, you fucking asshole!" Instinctively, Louie dashed toward the water to save Andy, but Stan sneered at Louie and demanded he not make a move to help. Without a second thought, Mom reeled back and threw a single punch that landed Stan on the ground, unconscious. At that, Louie proceeded to retrieve Andy and, at Mom's instruction, we all ran back to our house and got in the car. Mom called the police to report Stan. The last time I saw Stan, the police were cuffing him and putting him in the back of their cruiser. We drove away with Mom in the station wagon she stole from her mother. Ever the optimist, I clearly remember thinking that now, finally, Mom would be better and more devoted to us since Stan was out of the picture. I so much wanted this to be true.

Too Good to be True

We ended up at Parkwood Estates, a trailer park in Plant City, Florida. The trailer we rented was a basic two-bedroom style that came already furnished with a full living room and kitchen set, a full-size bed in one room, and a twin bed in the other. We even had a small black-and-white TV that, with the assistance of a wire coat hanger, could broadcast one local channel. This channel was so snowy that we could only watch it at night when there was enough contrast that we could make out some semblance of a picture. Pretty much the only shows we could get on that TV were Benny Hill and Carol Burnett, but we made it work.

Mom didn't know anyone in the area yet, so she occupied herself with motherly duties. Armed with buckets, scrub brushes, cleaning solutions, and a scarf Mom wore Rosie the Riveter-style, we got busy cleaning our new home. I was pleased with the effort Mom was making. Maybe the clean break from Stan hit some sort of refresh button for her. Maybe she finally saw our four little faces looking back at her in pleading desperation saying, "You're all we've got." We were off to a good start. This was the new beginning we all needed, and this time, I convinced myself, it was going to work.

Mom got us signed up for food stamps and we made a trip to the store where we stocked up on food that would fill our bellies. On our return, we worked together and put everything away—well, everything but a large sack of potatoes. We looked at those potatoes and saw a mountain of French fries, the same way Sylvester saw roasted poultry on a platter when he looked at Tweety Bird. Mom agreed to make French fries for us if we peeled the potatoes. Challenge accepted!

Louie and I, each equipped with a paring knife, set out to peel those potatoes. That just goes to show you that, with the right motivation—and a little Benny Hill theme music that we hummed to help drive the pace—kids will do anything, even race their sibling to get ten pounds of potatoes peeled.

One by one, Louie and I snatched potatoes from the sack; they still had Idaho earth on them. At a fever pitch we flicked our paring knives fast around each potato, at the expense of a knuckle or two. We were peeling so fast it looked like sparks were flying, but it was just the glint from our knife blades catching the light. Eric was excited too, but nobody trusted him with a knife, so he just jumped around the kitchen and rejoiced in our enthusiasm.

Before we knew it, every potato was peeled and sitting in the center of the table waiting for Mom to turn them into sliced, deep-fried, crispy-on-the-outside, fluffy-on-the-inside, greasy, salty goodness. And this time, Mom came through. We gorged ourselves on homemade French fries.

It wasn't long before Mom made a friend in the trailer park. Debbie lived nearby and was a single mom with three kids: a teenage daughter, Becky; Charlie, a preteen son; and Timmy, who was six. We knew to check over at Debbie's if we were looking for Mom; she was usually over there. Debbie shared with Mom her familiarity with the local resources available for financially strapped families.

I don't know what Mom signed up for, but soon we began receiving boxes of donations: books—adult romance novels—clothes, and non-perishable food. Once these donations started, our trips to the grocery store stopped. Now that we no longer *needed* the government-supplied food stamps, Mom would sell them to Debbie. The revenue she earned from her food stamp racket was used to fund her budget for cigarettes, beer, and drugs. It seemed that things hadn't really changed after all.

With all of Mom's money going toward her creature comforts, necessities fell to the wayside. Our electricity was turned off for non-payment on several occasions. When this happened, Mom would call the electric company and pose as a new resident, and the kind customer service agent would arrange to have a technician come out to connect the electricity. Then Mom would have one of us answer the door so they could gain access to restore power. This ruse worked for about thirty to forty-five days until the account became delinquent and our power was once again turned off. She employed the same tactic the next time with another one of us answering the door. After the second episode, the electric company figured out her deception and we were out of luck.

With no electricity there was no heat, and the evenings became chilly. Mom could have spent some of her money on another blanket or two; we only had two blankets, and when Eric or Andy wet one, we all had to move to the other bed with the other blanket. If they managed to wet the bed again, we were just screwed.

When four kids share a bed, no one really gets quality sleep. Someone is always tossing and turning, snoring, waking up thirsty, et cetera. One such night, thanks to someone's tiny bladder, we had to abandon the spacious double bed and settle in the alternate bed. This was always our last resort, as four kids simply don't fit comfortably in a twin bed. I helped whomever change into dry—probably not fresh—clothes, and we tried to find comfort in the overcrowded bed. Once we all got situated and back to sleep, the front door flew open and Mom stumbled in with some guy she brought home from a bar. They were doing that annoying loud drunken whisper where only they think they are being quiet. "Damn kids," Mom hissed. As soon as she got into bed with her new friend, she realized why we were all piled on the twin bed. She staggered back into our room. "Hey, you kids need to go to the other bed. I need this bed tonight." Mom's speech was slurred and her breath reeked of booze and cigarettes. She actually woke us up and threw us out of the bed.

I hated my life, and in my exasperation, I prayed for anything else. With one bed soaked and the other one occupied, we had nowhere else to go. We curled up on the floor like a litter of puppies and tried to force our way back to sleep, trying to ignore the carnal sounds coming from Mom and her friend on the tiny bed we wished we still occupied.

As Mom met other like-minded people, her old party-animal lifestyle resumed without missing a beat. When she was home with us, Mom would lie in bed either buzzed from alcohol, stoned from drugs, or both, and have me read to her from the donated, second-hand romance novels. I remember being so embarrassed when I had to read the steamy sex scenes out loud. While I was reading, it was Louie and Eric's job to rub her feet. They used to giggle at the embarrassing sex scenes.

When we were delinquent enough on the electric bill and the power was out, all the food in the refrigerator spoiled, which made our whole trailer reek. Mom wasn't home often enough to care about the stench; and when she was home, she wasn't lucid enough to notice. So Louie and I took it upon ourselves to empty out the fridge and clean the kitchen. We labored all afternoon to get everything perfect. When Mom came home, I proudly met her at the door. Beaming with pride I announced, "Look, Mom, we cleaned!" My arms were outstretched like those beautiful models who show off new cars as potential winnings on TV game shows. Since I was the thing that stood between her and the bed, Mom met my enthusiasm with a snarl and a swift backhand to the face. The power of her arm knocked me off my feet. With that, she went to bed and passed out.

When she wasn't down for the count or already out with whomever, she was primping the way she used to when she would go out with Aunt Barb. This was the only time she was sober and we could talk to her. We worked to keep her in a good mood by telling her how pretty she looked. We knew we were about to be locked in the trailer until her return. This wasn't as bad as it sounds. We enjoyed the freedom of not having to read smut books to her and massage her feet.

At first, Louie and I heeded her warning and didn't dare think about leaving home while she was gone. After all, she used a padlock on the only door and assumed that would hold us in.

Eventually, Mom would stay out a few nights at a time, and Louie and I grew bolder and learned that if we removed a few glass panes from the jalousie windows in the back of the trailer, we could make enough space to finagle our way free. We only used this technique to get to a neighbor's trailer so we could borrow some bread, milk, or maybe some sugar for water or, if we had it, Kool-Aid. And when we did leave, only one of us went while the other stayed home with Eric and Andy. It wasn't easy to get out, and it was even harder to get back in; once we got out of the window, it was about a six-foot drop to the ground. In order to get back in, we had to climb up a rotted-out tree stump that we kept nearby.

When Mom was gone for days on end, it was up to me and Louie to get everyone fed. We had a decent supply of canned food, but no can opener. Left with no other options, we employed a caveman technique with makeshift tools. Using a knife to cut into the top of the can as we pounded it with the bottom of another can, we gained access to our food. It was time-consuming and messy, but we proved that literally nothing is child-proof and that, most definitely, where there is a will, there is a way. Once we had liberated our dinner from the cans, we sat in a circle and ate. We each took turns eating one spoonful at a time. We'd munch on handfuls of dry Stove Top stuffing mix and pass around the canned green beans, new potatoes, pork and beans, and fruit cocktail in round-robin style until it was all gone and our tummies were satisfied.

On one particular evening when Mom left and we needed this or that miscellaneous item, it was my turn to go beg or borrow it from a neighbor. I had just got through the trailer's window and was walking across the way when I heard a car pull into the driveway. I was at the far end and had the benefit of being behind the trailer, so I wasn't in plain view of anyone in the driveway. Suspicious of anyone approaching, I turned to peek to see who was there. It was Mom retuning home. SHIT!

I was sure that if I was caught outside, I would receive a beating that my grandchildren would feel. There was no way to climb back into the trailer without being discovered. The re-entry process was far from graceful and quite loud as we shimmied up the side and wrangled our way back into the window. I'd surely kick the aluminum siding on the trailer, which would betray my clandestine mission.

Instead, I found shelter via an exposed seam in the trailer's aluminum skirting. I crawled, GI Joe style, under the trailer, trying to avoid the low-hanging wires and cables. It was dark and dirty under there, and who knows how many creepy crawly things were there with me, but desperate times call for desperate measures, and nothing I could encounter under the trailer could possibly be as horrifying as the wrath of Mom when I disobeyed.

Suddenly I was paralyzed. I couldn't move except for involuntary jagged motions. Gurgles, groans, and hissing sounds filled my ears, and then I realized that I had made contact with a live electrical cable and I was being electrocuted. Those sounds I heard were escaping my body as I was held captive there and the voltage coursed through me. *Well, isn't this just perfect*, I thought. *I'm going to die on this nasty-ass ground, under this nasty-ass trailer, while I'm hiding from that nasty-ass woman.* It wasn't until I heard a ringing in my ears that I was released from the paralytic power of the electricity. What seemed like minutes or even hours that I was being electrocuted, was actually only a few seconds. Had it been longer, I surely would have not survived, but my guardian angel was working overtime.

As luck would have it, Mom didn't stay long enough to notice that I was missing. She just stopped in to grab something, probably her overnight bag, and just like that, she was gone again. As I climbed out from under the trailer, I smirked and began to think I was invincible. I'd just survived being electrocuted.

Florida's warmth creates a hospitable atmosphere to grow citrus, lures senior citizens to retire in their golden years, and provides an extremely nurturing environment for insects. Without the frozen winter months that the states north of the Mason-Dixon Line endure, Southern insects are free to grow to near epic proportions, both in size and population. Cockroaches are about the size of an adult's thumb; mosquitoes are so rampant that trucks drive through neighborhoods on a weekly basis to spray poison; and spiders there are known as some of the largest in the nation.

One night, while I was in bed dreaming of a better life, one such spider emerged from whatever hiding place it called home and bit the back of my calf. The itchy bite area developed into a blister and then became swollen and very warm to the touch, indicative of an infection. It wasn't long before the blister started to ooze pus and blood. Up until now, my only real experience with bug bites was limited to mosquitoes. It wasn't until I started shivering and burning up at the same time that I decided to go to the school nurse for help. Thinking I just had a tummy ache, she walked me back to the sick room to lie down, and that's when she spotted the problem.

She saw the dried blood on the back of my jeans that directly corresponded to the open wound on the back of my calf. She noted how it was warm to the touch, and the black decay of flesh radiating from the original bite site. With the limited resources in her office, there was only so much she could do to help me. She carefully drew a circle around the perimeter of the inflamed area; any spread of the wound beyond this outline would help determine how rapidly the infection was spreading. She pulled out her most powerful weapon—the phone—and called the local clinic to schedule an appointment for me. Then she opened her desk drawer and pulled out a tablet upon which she jotted a note that I was to give to Mom. This note detailed the gravity of my affliction and provided my appointment information at the clinic.

The doctor at the clinic down the street identified the wound as a spider bite. This was not the work of an ordinary house spider. My leg, which looked more like a gunshot wound than a spider bite with its radiating heat, black center, and seeping yellow pus, had all the telltale signs of a brown recluse bite. This is about as bad as it gets when it comes to spider bites. The average spider bite is irritating, maybe itchy for a day or two, and it might even sting a little. But the brown recluse is in a different class, similar to comparing a bell pepper to a Carolina reaper pepper. The bite from this specimen will cause some serious damage.

Affected flesh decays and, left untreated, spreads. Its victims have been known to lose limbs and even their lives.

I had a standing weekly appointment to have the scab removed and thick green pus drained. These treatments included an injection of antibiotics right in the center of the bite area, which was an extremely painful gash of an open wound, and I dreaded going to the clinic for treatment. I protested the doctor each time as if I could possibly win. He was adamant that the scab had to be removed so the wound could be cleaned and treated, and he warned of dangers if it was not treated correctly. *Great!* I thought. *I've survived being hit by a car, brutal bullying from my peers and my own mother, and being electrocuted under that Godforsaken trailer, only to have an itty-bitty spider take me out.*

To make matters worse, the infected wound would ooze. Every time I wore jeans, the discharge would stick to my pant leg and dry. It adhered the denim to my leg like glue, and then when I took off my jeans the wound would rip open again. It was a slow and painful road to recovery, but I've been through worse. I have a lifelong scar and permanent indentation from this venomous spider, an added constant reminder of yet another traumatic event from my youth. But because of the intervention of skilled and sympathetic people who have been strategically placed in my life at the exact time I needed them most, I've always been able to fight my way back. I truly believe with my whole being that I was destined to endure and survive all these life experiences so I can do some good in the world and help others.

Devil Spawn of Parkwood Estates

At nine years of age, I was falling victim to the cruel joke of adolescence. The cuteness of childhood was waning, and I was losing the baby fat that makes kids adorable. My baby teeth were falling out and my new adult teeth were coming in, but they seemed too big for me. Eyeglasses always make for an easy target, and it didn't help that I was cross-eyed from the hit-and-run drunk driver back in Pennsylvania. My name throughout the trailer park was Cock-Eyes. I really don't think they even knew my real name, nor did they care to learn it. Kids can be so mean, and the kids who called Parkwood Estates home were especially evil. It made me think there was something in the water that reordered the firing sequence of their synapses and ultimately changed their personalities to little devil spawn.

One day, a gang of about five or six of these terrors circled around me and made it impossible for me to walk away. They jeered at me and called me Cock-Eyes as they pelted me with rocks. One girl picked up an enormous handful of mud and smeared it in my face. My only offense was looking different. They continued to tighten their circle, and I was completely helpless. I dropped to the ground and covered my head with my arms as I curled up into the fetal position. I could feel each rock as they landed with great force on my back, arms, legs, and head. I summoned all my strength, I could feel it start at my toes, and like a tsunami building momentum as it advances toward the shore, all my muscles contracted and my bodily functions ceased. I screeched at the top of my lungs for them to leave me alone and let me go. My out-of-body experience left me emotionally and physically exhausted; soon I felt a warmth flow over me. In the midst of my desperation I'd lost all control of my bladder.

This didn't dissuade these mutant-brained monsters. They continued with their assault until an adult who had heard my outcry began running to my rescue. My unfortunate physical reaction to this torture earned me a new moniker: Cock-Eyed Pissy Pants. To make matters worse, one of my attackers was Becky, Debbie's daughter. Since our moms were friends, it would have been nice if Becky had taken me under her wing like a little sister, but she had other plans.

Timmy, a six-year-old hellion everyone loved to hate, was Debbie's youngest. This kid was an obnoxious brat who truly deserved any retribution he got. Timmy would push the limits of humanity, and often, when the object of his annoying little antics had finally had enough, they would push back, literally. Timmy was the frequent recipient of plenty of well-deserved shoves, slaps, punches, and kicks. Being the brat he was, he would run home to his mommy whimpering and sometimes bawling about the "mistreatment" he received.

On one particular afternoon, Louie summoned me from our trailer, saying that Mom was over at Debbie's and was looking for me. Inside Debbie's trailer, I found her and Mom drinking beers. As Mom flicked ashes from her cigarette, she recounted how some girl who lived in our trailer park had hit Timmy. What Timmy failed to share was that he was the instigator and this girl was only defending herself. Since this girl was my age, Mom thought it best that I handle the situation, even though I didn't really know her, nor was I involved in the original scuffle. Obedient to Mom's command, off I went to find this girl and, in Mom's words, "kick her ass." As if I were a robot that was set in motion by some evil master programmer, I found this girl and chased her down. I reluctantly pinned her to the ground with my knees on her arms. I threw a few weak punches, well aware that Mom and Debbie were watching me. I knew I had to make it look good, but I really didn't want to hurt her. I was struck by the irony that only a few days ago I was enduring a brutal beating from bullies, and now here I was, repeating the cycle on this poor girl. Before long, I saw her father emerge from the manager's office and run toward us shouting. I didn't want to get in trouble for fighting and risk getting us evicted from the trailer park, so I stopped hitting her and ran back to Debbie's.

Feeling a sick sense of accomplishment, I returned to Debbie's trailer, certain that Mom would be pleased with me for successfully carrying out her orders. I let myself in, and as the screen door swung closed behind me, I announced with dread-filled triumph, "I kicked her butt, Mom, like you said." Opposing emotions swirled inside my head and heart. No matter how hard I tried, these emotions remained as incompatible as oil and water. I was conflicted by the sense of satisfaction for having completed Mom's demand, but at the same time, self-hatred attacked my soul for the willful betrayal of a fellow underdog.

Before I could attempt another failed effort to reconcile myself and my deed, Mom backhanded me right in the face. "You didn't draw blood," she snarled. Immediately, my eyes began to tear and blood poured from my nose. I ran home as blood dripped from my hands that were covering my face.

In the bathroom, I cleaned myself up and packed my nose with toilet tissue, hoping to stop the bleeding. I went to the bedroom and threw myself on the twin bed that I shared with my three brothers. The stench of the dried urine that marinated the mattress assaulted my senses.

My head was pounding from the impact of Mom's knuckles, and I was reeling from the reality of what had just happened. In that moment, all of my hopes for any kind of normalcy vanished. I stopped overlooking Mom's flaws. I stopped trying to fix her, placate her, or even make excuses for our unbearable living conditions. She was the reason for all of the misery in our lives, and I wanted her to die. I started fantasizing about getting her out of my life. Why couldn't I have been born into a family that had a normal mom—the kind where she hugged and kissed her kids every day and tucked them in bed every night? A mom who planned fun outings for bonding and enrichment and cooked fresh wholesome meals. I wanted what other kids at school seemed to have. What kind of adult, let alone a mother, orders her child to beat up another child for some trivial schoolyard incident, and then hits her child for not drawing blood?! I was done!

Eventually, Louie came in with a peace offering from Mom. She had handed him some food stamps and sent him to the store to buy me a candy bar, which I refused to accept. Louie was stuck in an impossible situation; he tried to keep the peace and avoid fueling Mom's animalistic behaviors, but at the same time, he could never alienate himself from me. He knew he was my only friend.

I thought it was cool to hang out with Louie and his friends because I didn't have anyone else. A year older than Louie, Charlie was the closest in age to him among all the boys in the trailer park, and therefore his best match for a playmate. Louie, Charlie, and another boy from the neighborhood often hung out together, playing and getting into typical mischief.

When it rained, they all sought shelter in one of our trailer homes. One fateful summer afternoon, we were all cooped up in our trailer, and of course, we lacked adult supervision.

Charlie returned from the bathroom holding something behind his back. The devilish grin on his face revealed that he had already schemed up some malicious plan for his entertainment. He held up a thick rubber bag with long tubing attached. At the end of the tube was a long nozzle. "Eww, gross, hahaha, look at this," he mocked as he swung the nozzle around by the hose. My memory flashed back to when I'd found this very same object under the bathroom sink when I was cleaning. I brought it to Mom and asked what it was. She looked up to see what I had, and in her usual matter-of-fact manner she told me it was her douche bag. Not satisfied with only a new term, I asked her what it was used for. She, again very indifferent, simply said, "That's what women use to keep their private parts clean." Now that I had a suitable answer, I was satisfied. I returned it to the bathroom where I'd found it and it never crossed my mind again. Until now. Trying to fit in with the older boys as their equal, I laughed and repeated what Mom had told me.

Out of the corner of my eye I saw Charlie make a nonchalant head nod toward me that, without a word, commanded the other kid to grab me. Louie was an unwilling participant. Moreover, he was oblivious to the plan and didn't pick up on the obvious clues; the disconnected expression on his face revealed as much. Charlie, the ringleader, kept yelling, "Get her arms, get her legs!" Together, the boys pinned me down and yanked off my shorts and panties.

"STOP! STOP! GET OFF ME!" I screamed as I tried to fight them away. But they were too strong. Charlie took the long nozzle of the douche and jammed it inside me as far as it would go. Immediately, white-hot pain coursed through my body, and I screamed out in sheer agony. Tears flooded my eyes and ran down my face; hot tears dripped into my ears.

I weaved between two worlds: my reality and an altered state I created to help me escape the terror. I remember questioning, *What kind of human being finds pleasure in inflicting such horrific pain on someone else? This guy must be a psychopath.*

The rape continued for what felt like eternity as Charlie kept shouting for Louie and the other boy to hold me down as he repeatedly thrust the nozzle in and out of me with great force. Frantic, I squirmed as much as I could, but I was no match for Louie and the other boy. Since I couldn't fight back with my body, I looked to the only other person I thought I could count on: Louie. As our eyes met, I conveyed all of my panic and bewilderment, fully expecting Louie to snap out of his follow-the-leader mentality. Louie met my plea with a look of shame. He simply didn't have the fortitude to stand up to Charlie and defend me.

In a desperate last attempt to end this attack, I summoned the last of my strength, and through tears and a cracking voice, I tried to shout, "Louie, no!" I thought that perhaps the desperate sound of my voice would shock him out of his trance and he would come to my aid.

One boy pinned my arms and the other pinned my legs. I was completely immobilized on the bed; the stench of dried urine compounded my misery, and I was incapable of breaking free. I squeezed my eyes tightly shut and thrashed my head violently from side to side. This was the only control I had over my body. The pain was so intense that my breath escaped me, and with it, my voice. When I did stop thrashing, I opened my eyes and saw Eric standing in the doorway.

Eric had no idea what was going on, but the terrified look on his face proved he knew it wasn't a game. Eric kept trying to leave the room, and Charlie screamed at him to help hold me down. He didn't or couldn't verbalize his response; he simply shook his head no. Tears welled up in Eric's eyes as he had to witness what was being done to me.

As the violence of the attack diminished, they turned their attention to exploration, almost as if they were doctors there to examine me. I resigned myself to the fact that I was alone and had no one to rescue me. I quit struggling against the boys and waited for the torture to end. Just as quickly as they had begun, they lost interest and stopped. As if they were using a magnifying glass to fry ants on the sidewalk, when they were done they simply walked away, leaving their victim alone to suffer.

Out of all of the misery in my life thus far, I point to this event as the turning point. It was here, during the excruciating rape, that I pivoted and became a fighter, no longer allowing anyone to make me a victim ever again.

Despite all the pain I had endured, what hurt me even more was that my confidant, my best friend, my protector and big brother offered me nothing but betrayal.

Louisville Slugger

I had no friends at the trailer park. I loved cats, but I was forbidden from having a pet because Mom said she was allergic. I used to find stray cats and sneak them home with me; they were my friends. As long as they stayed in the dresser drawer where I put them, all was fine. One cat I had wasn't exactly a stray. Muffin had a collar, but I found her roaming outside so I brought her home. She was a beautiful calico with white, orange, and brown markings, and she had an unusual pink nose that enhanced her unique beauty. Unfortunately, Muffin's temperament didn't match her appearance. This little cat was a meanie and escaped the first chance she got.

Another cat that I found was, in fact, a stray. I named her Precious. She was black with random white markings; she looked like the opposite of a Holstein cow. Unlike Muffin, Precious was sweet and would nuzzle up to me for a good cuddle. It seemed that we both needed this love and were blessed to find it in each other's company.

One afternoon I was outside playing with Precious. We were in our own little world of make-believe. I heard a desperate but familiar voice calling my name. This voice was so distant, it was almost dream-like. Soon, the disembodied voice became louder and more frantic as it approached. I looked up and saw Louie sprinting toward me and the trailer. He was screaming, "Sissy, Sissy, open the front door!" as his feet pounded on the ground and his hair bounced, then flopped to his forehead with each stride. Louie was being chased by boys from the trailer park, and I could tell this wasn't a game. Louie looked like he feared for his life. I imagined this was the same frantic expression I had when I looked to Louie for help during my rape.

A fleeting thought crossed my mind: *I should just run into the trailer and lock Louie out.* Show him the same betrayal he showed me not too long ago. He should feel firsthand the pain of the psychopath Charlie and his wicked sidekick. Above that, he should feel the bitter sting of betrayal.

Instead, out of compassion, I dashed to the trailer and opened the front door just in time for the two of us to run in and slam the door shut again. Inside with Louie, I tried to wrap my head around what was going on, but Louie was too winded to explain.

Trying to catch his breath, Louie's chest was heaving and he was gasping for air. Within moments, I heard the boys outside. They were shouting for Louie, throwing anything they could find, and kicking our flimsy aluminum front door. I watched, horrified, as each kick left a big dent. I feared they would break the door in. The more I heard the voices outside, the angrier I became. My blood began to boil. Adrenaline coursed through my body and gave me a surge of energy so strong that I felt like I could lift a car.

I ran to the bedroom and grabbed the Louisville Slugger we had found in a nearby wooded area. This bat was altered to do some major damage; it was embedded with long nails that protruded out the other side, and it looked like a medieval torture device. I threw open the front door, swinging the nail-studded bat and screaming as loud as I could: "Get the fuck out of here, you motherfuckers! I'm gonna fucking kill you!" I must have been a sight: cross-eyed, wielding a primitive-looking weapon, screaming threats I fully intended to bring to fruition. I can still remember the stunned look on the boys' faces as they turned to run away, shouting to each other about how crazy I was.

When my attention turned back to Louie, he was still panting and trying to recover from his near-death experience.

I knew that, for us, survival wasn't merely a game to play to ease boredom. The danger was real, and the stakes were high. If Louie wasn't going to assume the role of protector, I would.

Artwork by Eric G. Isaacs

Holiday Help

Given all the atrocities of home life, I viewed school as my salvation. Between the hours of eight a.m. and three p.m., I was afforded the opportunity to escape hell. I didn't have to defend anyone's honor, I didn't have to worry about finding food for me and my brothers, and I could simply get lost in the fantasy of being just another kid. But school was a luxury that wasn't always available.

Without electricity to operate an alarm clock, I relied on the voices of other children as they walked to the bus stop. When I heard this, I would jump out of bed, throw on one of a few pairs of shorts or the single pair of jeans I owned and a top, and dash out the door. I neglected the usual morning routine of bathing, brushing my teeth, or even running a brush through my hair. I was just elated that I got to go to school. Some days it was Louie's turn for school, and I would have to stay home to tend to Eric and Andy. Mom was nowhere to be found or not coherent enough to care for them.

As much as I liked going to school, I had plenty of experiences when I was bullied or labeled as an outcast by my classmates. Mandatory school lice checks revealed my infestation. In an effort to limit the exposure to the other kids, I would be segregated and forced to sit across the room from my classmates. There we sat, on opposing sides of the classroom, thus reinforcing the great divide that separated me from the anonymity of being average. Across from me sat Tiffany, the little girl with bouncy blond hair. She was always dressed in the latest fashion and was the poster child for "privileged." I hated her for what she had and who she was, but I also wanted to be her. She stared me down with judgment and disdain and called me names in mockery, as if the lice nesting on my scalp were somehow my choice.

The school year progressed, and I made it to class as often as I could. With Christmas approaching, I dreaded the long two-week break when I wouldn't even have the hope that I could go to school. Louie, Eric, Andy, and I soldiered on day by day. Mom would typically be absent, which was fine with me.

Even though we had our suspicions, we never actually saw Mom use drugs, until one day when she needed help shooting up. She recruited Louie to hold the rubber strap tight on her arm to stop the flow of blood and expose a vein. As soon as a vein popped up, she buried the needle and pressed on the syringe. The dose flooded her bloodstream and within an instant she drifted off. Her eyes, half closed, rolled backward, her jaw went slack, and she slumped back on the couch. Mom's narcotic-based escape no longer had an effect on me; I couldn't care less.

One day, we were quietly playing while Mom was passed out in bed. A knock on the door broke the near silence in the trailer. We scrambled to answer the door fast before Mom could wake up and we'd have to pay the price. Behind the door on the top step stood two ladies with big warm smiles. They were holding overstuffed bags full of food and Christmas presents. Evidently someone saw that we had a need and signed us up for holiday assistance from some local charity or church. Thank heavens for the kindness of strangers.

Expecting nothing for Christmas, the boys and I were overjoyed to receive something. The food items were of the standard, run-of-the-mill, non-perishable variety: boxed mac and cheese, stovetop stuffing mix, canned beans and vegetables, and the like. But the highlight of it all was the candy. We would have been happy to eat our fill of stuffing mix or canned beans, but what kids, especially starving kids, would reject a mountain of candy!

We looked at the candy, then looked at each other. No words were needed. We ripped open the bags like our very lives depended on it. All that could be heard throughout the trailer was candy wrappers and munching. It was a feast that rivaled even the grandest of Thanksgiving dinners. We ate so much so fast that soon we felt the full effect of what parents warn their children about on Halloween: we all had stomach aches. The hurried activity of scarfing down candy stopped, and the sounds of candy wrappers and eating were replaced with moaning and groaning. We held and rubbed our bellies, hoping that self-soothing would be enough to quiet our unhappy digestive tracts. But we were wrong.

Louie jolted up and out of the room; his hands covered his mouth as he dashed past me and into the bathroom. I heard the undeniable sound of vomiting, and I only hoped he made it to the toilet. I was pacing the room, hoping to walk off that nauseated feeling of too much candy. The sound of Louie barfing didn't help one bit. We passed each other as I sprinted into the bathroom, dropped to my knees in front of the toilet, and puked. The bitter taste of stomach acid mixed with the sweetness of candy and burned my throat on the way up. My body convulsed with such force as it expelled everything I had just gorged on. What a complete waste of all that delicious, chocolaty, nougaty, peanutty goodness. Eric felt sick too, but luckily he never threw up. After we recovered from the "revenge of the candy," we turned our attention to the Christmas presents.

Eric, who had just turned five a week earlier, was filled with the awe and wonder of Christmas. Jumping up and down, clapping his hands, he asked where all of the presents came from. With our own Christmas spirit brewing inside, and with no desire to rip the magic away from him, Louie and I gleefully told him it was Santa, of course. We ripped off the festive wrappings with gusto. We didn't get loads of toys or a Walkman or any of the other gifts coveted by kids our age; instead, we received gifts with definite utility: sweaters, scarves, socks, et cetera. But we felt like the richest kids on Earth, and we wore our new garments with pride.

We fell back into our routine in the weeks that followed Christmas and New Year's. I would get to school when I could. Whenever Mom would leave, she would give us the same instructions by way of a threat: "Do not leave home while I'm gone!" We heard the authority of the padlock snap shut as she locked us in. She jumped on the back of a motorcycle with some guy, and that was the last I saw of her. We were prepared for some time to pass before she returned home again. Hours turned into days, which turned into a week, then more. I'm not exactly certain how much time passed, but it was at least several weeks.

During this time, we maintained our humble existence. We hammered our way into the canned food and fought over the two threadbare blankets. The electricity was turned off and we were freezing. We would huddle together at night to stay warm. Before long, we had to ration our food. Mom had been gone longer than ever before, and we had no idea when to expect her back. We were in survival mode.

One night, in the middle of the night, we awoke to the sound of someone pounding on the door. Startled and terrified, we all huddled in the corner of one of the bedrooms. My mind raced. Who could possibly be out there in the dead of night? I was so terrified, I could hear my heart beating in my head. Was it an escaped convict looking for a place to hide, or a group of bandits coming to pillage, or Bigfoot? The possibilities were limited only by my imagination. I wished I had that dreadful Louisville Slugger at that very moment. The thought to go grab it crossed my mind, but it was in the other bedroom on the other side of the trailer, and I would have had to pass in front of the door to get there. Andy was so frightened by the deliberate and persistent sound that broke the silence of the night that he began to cry, and nothing we did would pacify him.

We didn't have to wait in horrified suspense very long. Soon the mystery people outside made their way into our home by kicking at the aluminum door until the bottom access panel gave way. My frantic question was answered, as what seemed like an army of men invaded our home. I heard a man's voice announce that they were the police. Strong beams of light from their flashlights blinded us in the darkness. As policemen entered our trailer, they found all four of us desperately clinging to each other in the corner of the front bedroom. Hot, salty tears streaked down my cheeks. Snot bubbled out of my nose. I was, like my brothers, inconsolable.

In our panic and desperation, we'd pulled blankets and pillows off the bed to cover ourselves. Three sets of wide eyes peered out from behind our ridiculous barricade. Andy was clinging to me in sheer desperation, crying so hard that he was on the verge of hyperventilating. Our arms and legs were firmly intertwined, and we were screaming and crying. In that moment, four separate kids morphed into a single being with a single purpose: to stay together.

One by one, the police forcefully separated and lifted us away from each other's frantic clutches and handed us to awaiting police officers outside. Andy was ripped from my arms. I felt like part of my soul had been snatched away.

I took it upon myself to be the spokesperson for the group. "Please just leave us alone! Our mom will be back soon, and we're not allowed to leave the trailer without her." But it was like I was speaking a foreign language. My desperate pleas fell on deaf ears. They probably explained that they were there to rescue us and take us somewhere safe, but I was out of my mind with panic and didn't hear anything but my own frantic petitions. I was the last one to be taken out, but I didn't make it easy for the officer. I was flailing my arms and legs in a last-ditch effort to be left alone. As I was being lifted up, I grabbed the ragged blanket that carried the stench of urine.

Once we were all outside, my head now throbbing from the adrenaline rush, we were placed in the back of police cars, the boys in one, and I in another. We drove for what seemed like eternity. I was all alone in the backseat of the police car, and my mind was still racing from the rescue mission. I tried to stay alert, making mental breadcrumbs so I could find my way home again. Given the stress of the night, the fact that I had been awoken from a sound sleep, and the sudden drop in adrenaline, I couldn't help but doze off.

We pulled up to a large plantation-style home, the kind you would see in *Gone with the Wind.* I was met at the door by a kindly older woman who wore a robe and slippers. She greeted me with a meek smile that I interpreted as pity—I hated that. I was ushered into the main front room of this large house. There were about five or six overstuffed couches in the center of the room and a most impressive grand staircase to my left. The opulent staircase boasted a rich oak finish and flared out at the bottom steps. My eyes were drawn all the way to the top, where I saw about eight teenage girls who had been roused from their slumber to see the new girl who would be joining them. It was a surreal feeling to have been whisked away from our trailer in the middle of the night and deposited in this home with all these girls watching me. Some grasped their blankets and pillows as if they had been teleported straight from their beds. As I stood there on the ground floor with the house mother, I thought, *Now what?*

Misfit Toys

There I stood, clutching that pathetic, urine-soaked blanket. The house mother apologized for not having any hot food to offer, but she took me by the hand and gently led me into the kitchen to see what she could whip up. "I would love a peanut butter and jelly sandwich," I replied when she asked me if I wanted anything to eat. Before I knew it, I was sitting in the kitchen with her, halfway through a PB&J sandwich made just for me.

What a surreal feeling to have my very own food. I didn't have to share it with my brothers, and I didn't have to ration it to make it last for many days. The glass of milk was nothing short of heavenly, and I drank every drop. A filet mignon couldn't have satiated me more. Since our electricity was off, we hadn't had milk in a very long time.

I could feel my body reviving as the nourishment enriched me, the way a wilted flower perks up when it gets water. My eyes felt as if they'd brightened, color returned to my sullen cheeks, and I gained the strength to straighten my posture. It was as if God sent an angel to breathe life back into my feeble body, which was slipping away and had all but given up. The house mother stayed with me as I gobbled up the food she provided. I wondered what she thought as she sat there watching me. Did she know all of the horrible details of the past few weeks? Was she aware of what circumstances had led me to her tender care? Could she tell how grateful I was for her compassion?

As I finished my first meal in weeks, the house mother explained that I needed to get cleaned up before I could go to bed; the squalor we were living in offered nothing but a headful of lice and an outbreak of ringworm. I bent over the sink as she gently washed my long blond hair and rinsed it with a handheld showerhead that was attached to a long hose. The medicated lice shampoo burned my inflamed scalp on contact. I could feel the surviving parasitic insects on my cheeks as they tried to escape their impending doom. As she rinsed my hair, I opened my eyes and watched with morbid curiosity as the sudsy water streamed off my head into the sink. The water was black with dead and dying lice. It looked like a black river flowing into the sink and swirling down the drain.

The next step in the delousing process was to secure a shower cap over my hair to suffocate the remaining unwanted tenants. After a warm bath, I got to go to bed for what was left of the night. The sleeping area was a large room with rows of metal bunk beds lining the walls. It reminded me of the sleeping quarters you see in a military genre movie when the cadets arrive for basic training: cold and impersonal. While there were lots of girls in those beds, many were unoccupied. I climbed into one of the available bunks and stared into the room full of sleeping girls. I wondered if my brothers were in a similar room. After what felt like hours, I finally allowed myself to drift off to dreamland.

In the morning, I was introduced to a second house mother. Both ladies were the embodiment of compassion and genuine kindheartedness. All of the defenses I'd been building up since the rape, the mental ramparts that protected me, the force fields, all of it just melted away when I looked into their eyes. For me, eyes have always been the one physical feature that reveals so much about a person's character. Are they kind and compassionate? Are they self-serving or even cold and calculating? I look into a person's eyes and I'm able to sense their intentions. Through their eyes, these two ladies invited me to be me, the tender little girl who, like a steel ball in a pinball game, had been bounced around, ricocheted here and there, used for folly and torture. I looked into their eyes and saw the souls of two genuinely compassionate and caring women. I saw lifetimes worth of wisdom and concern. It looked like these women wanted to absorb my pain and make me whole again. I transformed from an armadillo with hardened armor into a delicate but still strong spider web as a result of the kindness in their eyes.

The ladies assured me that Louie was being cared for on the boys' side of the campus, and Eric and Andy were in an area designated for younger children. They asked what I liked to eat for breakfast, so I listed everything that I liked and, like a wish granted by my fairy godmother, I got everything I asked for. I devoured a bowl of cereal, pancakes, and biscuits and gravy. I washed it all down with a tall glass of milk. All the while I was fearful that at any moment Mom would storm in and take me away, so I knew I had better enjoy it while it lasted. Every time the phone rang or the front door opened, my heart skipped a beat, terrified that it could be her to take us back to hell.

After breakfast, I spent many hours trying to sit still while one of the house mothers had the tedious chore of combing through my hair with a lice comb. This process was necessary to remove all of the unhatched eggs still clinging to my hair. My head was sore from microscopic bites and constant scratching to relieve my itchy scalp, and now the tugging as the narrowly spaced comb's teeth separated each hair as it raked through my mop was almost more than I could bear. It was a wonder she didn't just spare herself the effort and me the anguish and shave my head.

At nine, I was the youngest girl in the house; the next youngest girl was fourteen. These girls treated me like a baby doll. They dressed me in their clothes, which were too big, and they brushed and braided my hair. I was their breathing, walking doll. I began receiving daily treatment for the ringworm, and with a little cajoling, I was convinced to surrender my blanket to be laundered, which it desperately needed.

Life wasn't bad in the children's home. I was clean and fed. I had my own bed and new friends who truly understood me because they each had similar backgrounds. After a few days in the plantation-style home, I was assigned to one of the many ranch houses on the grounds. Each house had two bedrooms with two bunk beds in each for the girls, and one bedroom for a house mother who oversaw the welfare of the girls in her care. She would make us breakfast in the mornings, and then we went off to school, which was held in modular homes on the campus.

During school hours, I was reunited with Louie as all the children attended school together. Once we finished our page of arithmetic or spelling, we had free time. The modular homes were sectioned off into various stations, each containing a different activity. Louie and I would spend our time at the station containing a portable record player, which was built into its own white carrying case. This record player could only accommodate 45s, and there were only three records there to play: the Go-Go's *We Got the Beat*, Survivor's *Eye of the Tiger*, and Joan Jett's *I Love Rock and Roll,* but we loved to sit and listen to these songs over and over again. Other times we would sit on the floor and just talk about how much we liked it at the home and our mutual fear of Mom coming back to get us.

We ate lunch in the school's modular homes, and we were allowed to return to our group homes before dinner. At dinner time, we all went to the cafeteria escorted by our house mothers. This was the only other time that all the school-age kids got to be together. With compartment food trays in hand, we approached the food line. There were always several entrée options from which we could choose.

As we settled down at our tables to eat, I remember scanning the room and being struck by the number of kids who were sheltered in this facility. There had to be at least 100 kids in there eating dinner, not counting the younger ones who were kept separate from us. Each one of us had unimaginable baggage and trauma in our personal histories—the kind of baggage that would mold us for better or worse into the adults we would become. I compared us to the misfit toys that inhabited that special island in the Christmas TV classic—*Rudolph*. How many of us were doomed to repeat the cycle with our own children, and how many of us would have enough fortitude to change our destiny? Some of the kids were only temporary residents while their families corrected whatever problems they had or while they were awaiting extended family to claim them. Other kids were fated to age out in the system. I do respect the nature of anyone willing to adopt newborn infants, but there is a real need to increase adoptions of older kids.

We weren't at the children's home for more than a few weeks when an employee from the county child welfare agency came and loaded me and my three brothers into a van. The last time I had seen Eric and Andy was in the trailer when they were being ripped from my arms. It was great to be reunited with them. They looked clean, plump, and healthy. It was explained to us that we were being placed with a foster family. My heart was filled with mixed emotions. At least we weren't being taken back to Mom, but at the same time, we were just getting acclimated to life in the children's home. What would this new family be like? We didn't have many good familial experiences, and I couldn't imagine anything beyond the scope of our personal histories.

Pinch Me, I'm Dreaming

With my nose pressed against the window of the van, I watched as we entered a suburban community in Brandon, Florida. I looked in awe at the large homes with well-manicured lawns. Were we lost? This was so far removed from my wildest dreams that I simply couldn't fathom a lifestyle that matched the surroundings.

Soon we pulled into the driveway of a beautiful home, and before all four of us could free ourselves from the confines of the van, Ginger and Warren O'Donnell stepped out of their home to greet us. Ginger was a petite lady with curly red hair, and Warren was tall with salt-and-pepper hair. This couple had already raised their family and had the means to help others, so they dedicated themselves to helping underprivileged kids. They welcomed us with sincere embraces, and I immediately felt like I was home. Ginger and Warren gave us a tour of their home, and I got to see my bedroom. I had my very own bedroom! The entire house was lovely, but when we got to the backyard and I saw the in-ground pool complete with a diving board, I just couldn't wait to jump in and splash around. But that dip in the pool would have to wait; we were going on a shopping trip for new clothes. I was so excited. I couldn't remember the last time I had brand-new clothes. Everything had been from charity and nothing ever fit right. Back in the trailer, my only pair of jeans were so tight that I had to lie on the bed just to get them zipped.

We pulled up to K-Mart, and I couldn't believe my eyes! This place was huge and everything was shiny and new. *Are we at the mall?* I wondered. I'd never seen anything so impressive. Warren and Ginger let me pick out my own clothes. I distinctly remember one particular outfit as my all-time favorite. It was a royal blue jumper with three-quarter-length sleeves and capri-length pant legs with yellow ruffles and cuffs that accented the sleeves and legs. This jumper was my absolute favorite possession, and I felt so pretty when I wore it. Eventually Ginger gently encouraged me to broaden my wardrobe, as I always gravitated to this jumper when left to my own devices.

That K-Mart shopping trip is a fond memory not only because I got brand-new clothes, but because I also got to pick out my very first Walkman. It wasn't too fancy and didn't have all the bells and whistles like a cassette player, but it had all I needed: an AM/FM radio and my own personal earphones. I picked the blue one because blue was my favorite color. That way, Louie and I wouldn't mistakenly use each other's.

Music has always been the one constant throughout my life. I use it as entertainment, an escape from reality, a form of self-expression, and a way to mark the passage of time. And the earphones meant that my music was *my* music. I could listen to what I wanted, when I wanted it. Born in the hearts and souls of musicians, recorded in a far-off studio, broadcast by countless radio stations that beamed the songs through the airwaves to my Walkman, through my headphones, into my head to fortify my soul—I had an instant connection to the artists and millions of fans alike.

It didn't take long for me to take full advantage of my new surroundings. I acclimated to life in the neighborhood well and enjoyed my newfound freedom. This wasn't the adult role, the duty-bound "freedom" that obliged me to dash across a four-lane highway for bread and milk, or play unsupervised in a trash dumpster, but the relaxed childhood freedom that allowed me to plug in to my Walkman and joyfully explore my new neighborhood.

Armed with fresh batteries in my personal stereo, I would set out for long walks; I didn't even need shoes. I distinctly remember Billy Idol singing about a White Wedding as I kept the rhythm with my stride, boldly planting my feet squarely in the center of each sidewalk square, mindful not to step on a crack—I never knew why this was important, but I'd always heard to never step on a crack. I didn't care that I stubbed my toes on rocks or scuffed the bottom of my feet. Oh, the skin and blood I left in my wake as I paraded through the neighborhood with my tunes! It didn't matter how hot I got in the Florida heat. I had unlimited access to the pool at home as long as Warren or Ginger were there to supervise.

Soon we established a daily routine. Warren and Ginger worked full time, and Louie and I would ride the school bus to and from school each day. Eric and Andy stayed home with the babysitter. Eric had been registered in kindergarten, but his severe ADHD, a by-product of fetal alcohol syndrome, created an out-of-control little boy and ultimately got him expelled from school. This behavior took its toll on the babysitter also. As Louie and I walked home from the bus stop, we could only imagine what havoc Eric had created that day. It was commonplace for us to find him standing in the corner, serving hard time for whatever chaos he'd generated. Before homework, before a dip in the pool, Louie and I focused our energy on engaging Eric in an activity that would alleviate the babysitter's stress level. Our go-to resource was always a fun-filled game of Uno. Eventually, Eric's shenanigans wore down the babysitter and we found ourselves with a new one, again and again. On a few occasions, Ginger had to stay home from work because whatever babysitter we had at the time just needed a mental health day.

Although I enjoyed having my own bedroom and

watching MTV, perks that the O'Donnells afforded us, the private pool was my favorite advantage. I loved to simply float on my back and look up at the sky. I felt so peaceful as I floated weightlessly while the refreshing water supported and splashed me. I could easily have spent hours there, only leaving the pool to attend school. Louie and I occupied the deep end while in the shallow end Warren and Ginger systematically taught Eric and Andy how to swim, forever gifting them with a lifesaving skill. The first lesson was learning to put their faces in the water, and then how to blow bubbles. Soon they mastered the doggie paddle, kicking, and the freestyle stroke. They were regular little tadpoles. Pool time was everybody's favorite family activity, a far cry from the "swimming lesson" Andy's dad had imposed on him that infamous day at the golf course.

One afternoon, Ginger came out of the house holding the cordless phone. She called me over to the pool's edge and knelt down to talk to me. "Honey, I have your mom on the phone and she wants to talk to you," she said.

I squinted up at her. My mom? The sun's powerful rays blinded me as the dripping chlorine water burned my eyes. I was just beginning to believe that Mom was long gone, and I'd never see her again. Honestly, I had written her off the very moment she backhanded me for not drawing blood in the score she commanded me to settle back at the Parkwood Estates trailer park.

I was in the middle of registering the reality of Mom finding us after several months in the children's home and now with the O'Donnells when Eric broke into a full-fledged happy dance. He had overheard Ginger saying Mom was on the phone, and he squealed with delight at the opportunity to talk to her. Ginger handed him the phone. "Mommy! Hi, it's me, Eric. I love you, Mommy. When are you coming to get us?" Eric's innocent pleasure at the notion that this monster wanted back in our lives sickened me. He was too young to realize how abusive and negligent she was.

We passed the phone around and each of us spoke with her. "Hi, Baby." The disembodied voice on the other end was talking to me like nothing had happened. "I have a few things to take care of, then I'm coming to pick you up," she said.

Oh crap, I thought. I'd rather be raised by wolves than spend an hour with her.

Even though I seriously doubted her supposed intention of reclaiming us, that old familiar sickness washed over me. *What if she really does come back to get us?* After all we'd been through, would the state of Florida even grant her custody? I felt as though I'd been kicked in the gut. I handed the phone back to Ginger, climbed out of the pool, and escaped back to my room where I buried my head in my pillow and sobbed.

As far as I could tell, the O'Donnells enjoyed us as much as we enjoyed them. They got to stave off the empty nest syndrome and help needy kids in the process. We had the benefit of healthy meals, stability in our home environment, and regular attendance at school. I was beginning to let my guard down a little, but every time I did, I'd get that familiar knot in my stomach. Eric's acting out was an issue. The number of babysitters who resigned because of his hyperactivity was a real concern for me. I never could fully abandon my mother hen persona. I felt this even more intensely when Ginger had to call off work to take care of Eric and Andy when no other childcare options were available.

All good things have to come to an end, but I wasn't ready for my time with the O'Donnells to end. Not long after wrapping up the fourth grade, we packed up and left the lap of luxury. I remember crying and clinging to Ginger for dear life. She was crying too. If our leaving was such a hardship on her, why did we have to leave? My suspicion was that Eric's behavior was more than they had bargained for, and they were running out of reliable childcare options. Louie, Eric, Andy, and I climbed into the car of a county social worker, and we were on our way to a new foster family. I didn't care where we ended up. I wanted to stay with Warren and Ginger, but at least we weren't being sent back to Mom.

Eric, age five

The Lariscys

Seven miles isn't very far unless you're a kid; then, it may as well be halfway around the world. Seven miles is what separated us from the O'Donnells, but it was far enough to be a whole different town. Soon we pulled up to a brick ranch-style house in Dover, Florida. A modest, rural home was the backdrop for our new foster parents who stood in the driveway with huge smiles on their faces. Jerline and Henry Lariscy welcomed us and introduced themselves. Jerline had a strong Southern drawl, and she was short and pleasantly plump with curly black hair that was perfectly styled. Henry had a slight Southern accent. He was slender with a hint of a beer belly, and his green-and-white ball cap concealed his hair or lack thereof. They seemed nice enough, but I was leery of attaching myself to a new family, and I'd be damned if I was going to get hurt again. I was quickly building a wall to protect my heart.

The Lariscys had two handsome sons: sixteen-year-old Henry Junior, dubbed Lil' Henry, and fourteen-year-old Randy. Crystal, their adorable two-year-old daughter, had red hair and a fiery temperament to match.

Lil' Henry was the more serious and clear-headed of the two brothers. He had coal-black hair that he wore in a mullet, quite stylish in the '80s. I had a gigantic crush on him and liked to watch when he went out back to work on his prized green Mustang. The mischievous, playful, and always-up-to-something Randy was blond and very cute, but he delighted in picking on us and teasing us—typical big brother style. Crystal was the family doll baby and the quintessential pageant princess. As the only daughter, she was adored and doted on by the whole family.

The Lariscy home was kept very tidy, and Jerline had to be one of Elvis' biggest fans. Among her memorabilia she had an Elvis lamp, a two-foot ceramic Elvis figurine, and of course, the obligatory velvet Elvis portrait. I rarely saw her without makeup, and she always maintained a fresh manicure. She worked as a school bus driver for handicapped children. When Jerline was off duty, she kept the bus parked by the side of the house. I'm not certain what Henry's full-time job was.

Behind the house was a cow pasture where Bessie the cow lived, and behind that was the strawberry field where Henry spent much of his time when he wasn't at work. Like it or not, we were "home." Home was a one-story house of natural white brick. We had full range of the nearly one acre of land, excluding Bessie's pasture and the strawberry field. There were lots of trees to climb, including a huge oak tree that, based on its size, had surely stood witness to the Civil War. Only one tree was off limits: the weeping willow. Naturally we were drawn to the forbidden tree like Eve was drawn to the apple. We would grab a handful of its droopy branches and swing, Tarzan-style. As sure as the sun rises in the east and sets in the west, we landed in time-out for our crime against that protected willow.

Bessie grazed in her pasture every day, and when we played in the backyard, she was able to keep a watchful eye on us. Like the cats at Parkwood Estates, I claimed Bessie as my special friend. When I stood at the pasture fence and called her name, she would trot over to me. The cowbell around her neck clanked all the way. We had a special friendship; when I wasn't visiting her inside the pasture, I would reach my arm in from the outside of the enclosure to stroke her beautiful brown-and-white face. The feeling was mutual, and Bessie trusted me enough to eat from my hand. Not everyone got this privilege. Her long, sandpaper-textured tongue would graze my hand as she lapped up the fistfuls of grass I plucked for her. Compared to the rough surface of her tongue, Bessie's nose and lips were smooth and velvety, and I much preferred this to her tongue. Nevertheless, I was happy to bond with Bessie and simply wiped my hands on my shorts when she was done.

One day, Bessie wasn't acting like herself. "Moo... Mooo... Mooooo..." she bellowed. Panicked, I sprinted across the yard and into the house.

"Something's wrong with Bessie," I screamed as the door slammed behind me.

The Lariscys ran out to her pasture with me. "Oh, she's fine, honey. She's just fixin' to have her baby," Mom Lariscy explained.

Her what?! I didn't even know that she was pregnant.

Bessie became a mother right in front of me. I watched in awe, wonder, childlike innocence, and morbid curiosity as the calf squeezed out. Intuitively, Bessie turned toward her newborn and licked away the amniotic sac and fluid. The calf was curled up on the ground with her little legs tucked under her wet body. Soon a gangly hind leg, then the other emerged from under the calf. She tried with all her might to straighten them and lift the heft of her frame. Wobbly and very cautious, she began to raise her back end. Before long, her front half obeyed her natural instinct. Unsteady and shaky, she stood on all fours for a moment or two then, plop, she collapsed to the ground. What a jolt to her little newborn body. She soon tried it again, and after some physical exertion, the calf was up on all fours once more. But in a few moments, she was down again.

Witnessing this made me want to somehow channel all my strength into her. I knew she could do it. On her third or fourth attempt, the new calf was standing all on her own. I was so proud of her. Seeing this reminded me of when Andy learned to stand on his own and how I worked with him to teach him to walk. His little hands tightly grasped my first two fingers as I towered above him while he tried out his little legs. I named the new calf Betsy, and I couldn't help but love her.

While the Lariscy household provided for our needs, it was obvious that we, as the foster kids, were at the bottom of the family hierarchy. Certain rules were imposed on us while the Lariscy children enjoyed much more freedom. Rules like: needing to ask permission before we could take a snack from the refrigerator, and the even more unreasonable rule that we couldn't have a beverage with meals. We had to wait until after the meal was finished, all the while watching the ice melt in our drinks that were set deliberately right out of reach. As fate would have it, Louie and I were assigned to cleanup duty after dinner. Always looking for life's silver lining, we would eagerly gulp down the leftover sweet tea from everyone's glasses while we were in the kitchen alone cleaning up.

In addition to kitchen duty after dinner, we had to wash Jerline's school bus every weekend. This wasn't as bad as it sounds, because we had fun splashing in the garden hose. What a refreshing chore in the sweltering Florida heat.

The instant addition of four more rambunctious kids to the house was quite noticeable. Jerline probably couldn't hear herself think. She all but locked us out of the house most days and we were sent out in the heat and humidity to play. The only exception to this rule was if we got in trouble for something, we were summoned back into the house to sit in the corner for time-out. Even though time-out was punishment, at least we were in the comfort of air conditioning. Alas, it didn't take Jerline long before she wised up to our scheme and soon even our time-out punishment was outside. To add insult to injury, Louie, Eric, Andy, and I were forced to endure our time-out separated from each other, strewn to the farthest corners of the very yard we loved to play hide-and-seek in. Because of the yard's magnitude, it became our downfall during punishments. We were hot and thirsty, and the water spigot on the side of the house beckoned us with promises of cool refreshing water on obscenely hot summer afternoons. The only caveat was that one had to possess a soul with great fortitude, enough to risk being caught slinking away from our exile.

Maybe Jerline was always just at the right place at the right time, but Andy's shenanigans always seemed to capture her attention and test her nerves more than the rest of us. "ANDY! Don't do that! AAAAANDY! Stop touching that! ANDYYYYY! Leave that alone!" As days stretched into weeks, I grew more and more irritated at the way Jerline would shout at Andy. "Are you listening to me, boy? Why don't you answer me? Can you hear me, boy?" He would sit and blankly stare at her without responding or even a head-nod acknowledgment.

By now Andy was nearly three years old and by all standards should have been able to follow simple and even complex commands. The absence of any reaction to Jerline's increasing volume would infuriate her beyond reason. "Stop yelling at him!" I would shriek. I didn't like her and didn't like living there, so I had nothing to lose when I disrespected her.

Perhaps, if we were lucky enough, she would send us back to the O'Donnells' house.

Maybe I did receive preferential treatment over my brothers, or maybe my adult perspective has softened my memories over the years, but Jerline did take steps to improve my life. Her work with handicapped children heightened her awareness and sensitivity toward kids with special needs, and I was still cross-eyed from the hit-and-run drunk driver back in 1981. Sensing that I would face unnecessary ridicule from my new classmates in the fall, Jerline made it her mission to push the children's social services agency to approve corrective surgery for me before I started the fifth grade. Her crusade was successful, and I was checked into the local hospital for surgery.

I was admitted the evening before surgery so I could be prepped and ready first thing the next morning. Alone and bored in my hospital room, I finally saw an opportunity to make contact with the O'Donnells, so I reached for the local phone book and looked up Warren and Ginger. Before long, I was pouring my heart out to Ginger, who patiently listened to my grievances on the other end of the line. I visualized Ginger sipping on lemonade and dipping her toes in the pool as I prattled on about this or that injustice, never once recognizing the space between the proverbial rock and the hard place where I left her. Nor had I considered the Herculean task that Jerline and Henry had willingly accepted and imposed upon their family when they opened their doors to us. The "yes" they said to us essentially doubled their household.

Four little kids with lots of baggage desperately needed Jerline's brand of tough love but didn't even know it. Ginger lent a sympathetic ear, but my deepest wish did not materialize: she did not offer to come and rescue us.

My only memory after surgery was Randy carrying me in from the car to my room where I slept off the remaining effects of anesthesia. My eye was bloodshot and my vision was blurry for about a week, but I finally had two eyes that followed my commands, and I could no longer be called hurtful names and be harassed for looking different.

Not too long after that, the Lariscy household was visited by a social worker from the county's children's services agency. I could only hear bits and pieces of their conversation from the other room, but I knew full well the purpose of the visit. Shortly after the social worker left, Jerline shouted from the living room, "Who reported us to child welfare?"

I charged from the back of the house. "I did! Because you are mean and hateful! We don't like it here, and we want to go back to the O'Donnells' house," I declared. My punishment for my bravery and boldness landed me in the kitchen organizing all of the canned food in the cabinets. I toiled away at this tedious and meaningless task as my whimpering escalated to crying, which escalated to sobbing. Between each sob, I bemoaned my wretched state and professed my displeasure with their inane parenting style. The more I balked, the louder they laughed at me from the living room, and the more intense my wailing became.

Eventually I was done with the chore at hand, but I was far from finished with my temper tantrum. I stomped off to my room. On the way, I stopped in the living room and, as if she needed further proof of my misery, I shouted three regrettable words: "I HATE YOU!" Stomping down the hall to my room, I flung myself on the bed and continued sobbing and wailing into my pillow. As the evening grew into nighttime and all the other children went off to bed, Jerline and Henry settled into the TV room to unwind with an episode of *Dynasty* or *Dallas* or whichever show was on that night.

By this time I'd had time to calm down and consider where I came from and what I was gifted with in the Lariscys. Gone were the days of one-room apartments, bars, lumber yards, and trash dumpsters for playgrounds. I had a bed all to myself. I had meals, lessons, and structure. I had the luxury of going to school every day, and now I was one of the kids I'd envied not too long before.

I slinked around the corner and caught Jerline's eye. "I don't hate you," I said, my voice quivering with remorse. I delivered a heartfelt apology for my tantrum and hoped that I didn't ruin our chances of staying with the Lariscys.

Jerline met my apology with warmth. "Aww, I know you don't, honey." I ran into her arms for one of her legendary warm embraces. It was that very night that I began calling her Mom.

As the culture shock wore off, I began to warm up to the Lariscys. They really weren't bad people, just vastly different from our original foster family experience with the O'Donnells. I slowly began to realize that children need rules, boundaries, and discipline, and we came from a long history of lacking all of that. Years later, in high school, I was reminded of this in Newton's Third Law of Motion: For every action, there is an equal and opposite reaction; and dare I add "proportionate consequence." This lesson was one that I needed to reflect on quite often, especially in the beginning. Every time I had been reprimanded, scolded, and redirected, my knee-jerk reaction was to bristle against Jerline. I didn't fold the laundry correctly—if you want it done some special way, then you do it—or I didn't set the table on time—then get someone else to do it—or I didn't start my homework when I was told to—who cares, homework is stupid. The calmer, more rational me always came back with the subtext: *Jerline loves me and is trying to make me into a better person.*

Crystal Lariscy, two years old

The Monster Within

The Lariscy house was an uncomplicated, one-story home with a modest front porch. Because of the rural location, they had a sizeable yard compared to suburban counterparts. The floor plan was open and welcoming, and the living room, kitchen, and dining room were readily available. The only wall that dissected the area was a half wall that functioned as a counter dividing the kitchen from the dining room. This is where the boys and I sat for meals. The den, where the family TV stayed, was an after-market addition to the house and was separated by a sliding glass door that used to lead to the patio. This door was left in place and served as a convenient barrier from the TV room and the rest of the house. The house had a master bedroom with a full bathroom for Henry and Jerline, and two other bedrooms and one more bathroom for the rest of us. It was a tight fit, but I don't recall anyone complaining—too much. The boys' room had two bunk beds to accommodate Lil' Henry, Randy, Louie, and Eric. Crystal slept in a crib in the master bedroom with Henry and Jerline. That left me and Andy to share a room.

Sharing a room with a toddler is worse than it sounds. Every morning I would awaken to Andy's distracted quiet chatter. Lifting out of sleep, I could hear that he was up to something, but what, I couldn't tell. As I rolled over and peered down from my top bunk, I could see by the dawn, muted through our bedroom curtains, that he'd done it again. Every square inch of the bedroom floor was covered in clothes. Andy had entertained himself by emptying the entire dresser. I felt something snap inside and a monster emerged.

I would reflexively throw something at Andy to get his attention and make him stop. I'd throw my head back down to my pillow in disbelief and sheer angst that he'd done it again. As I took a few seconds to fully awaken and bemoan my current situation, I could hear Andy busying himself, gleefully jibber-jabbering as he sat in the middle of ground zero. Adrenaline would course through my nervous system and compel me to leap out of bed like a panther. Motivated by fear of being evicted by the ultra-neat-freak Jerline, I knew she wouldn't stand for a messy bedroom. We had a good thing here at the Lariscys, and I wasn't about to let Andy mess it up for us.

I'd land nearly on top of Andy and smack his hand until he dropped what he was holding. Andy always started to cry from being hit. The monster within me would clasp my hand over his mouth. Crying would wake Jerline and alert her to a problem in our room, and I didn't need her to come in and see the mess. Muzzling Andy's cries also restricted his ability to breathe, so I took him just to the brink of a crisis and then lifted my hand long enough for him to catch his breath.

Through a clenched jaw, I would command Andy to shut up. "Are you going to stop crying?" I would ask, my voice low and sinister. Andy had tears streaming down his face and snot running from his nose over my hand that was still covering his mouth. "You better shut up, SHUT UP! Do you hear me?" I would growl. My eyes reduced to narrow slits and I shook my finger in his face. My long hair hung in front of him. As if proximity could better transmit my fury, I drew his face so close to mine that I'm sure he could feel my hot breath on his cheeks as I scorned him. Andy's blue eyes were wide with terror; I knew he knew this wasn't a game.

When I withdrew my hand from his face, Andy softly wept. As I busied myself with the task of cleaning up Andy's mess, his fear of me escalated until it would crescendo to the point of sobbing. Chest heaving, he would suck his bottom lip in and out in sync with his sobs. When his volume reached a point of concern, I would grab his shoulders and shake him. "Shut up! Just shut up, you little brat!" *I could end you here and now*, I thought to myself.

My inner monster had taken control of my body, and I was a mere vehicle to deliver its blind rage. *What a little terror*, I would think as I finished cleaning up his mess. *Why the hell can't he just stay in bed and leave his grubby little hands out of the dresser?*

When all the clothes were picked up and put away, I would climb back into bed and try to fall back asleep until the rest of the family woke up. Although I'm convinced that my raw fury was the same feeling that Mom had when I was her target, never once while I was tormenting and terrorizing Andy did I see a parallel between myself and Mom. With Mom, my sheer existence was enough to set her off. In my conscious memory, I never did anything to instigate her wrath. It was quite the opposite: I worked to appease and soothe her. Even though I recognize that Mom and I each took different paths, we both arrived at the same point—out-of-control, animalistic rage that could only be spent, not squelched.

Was this suggestive of nature or nurture? The question burns inside me. Did I erupt like this because I learned such behavior from Mom, and she from her mom, or is there some nefarious gene in my DNA? My best hope is for the former, because if it is a learned attribute, then it can be unlearned or at least controlled.

In the heat of the moment, I had tunnel vision for the cause and effect of Andy's actions. I only saw the chaos that he created, the job of restoration that was left up to me, the sleep I was conceding, and the anxiety of losing the foster family and the only mom I'd ever really chosen to love. I wonder if, in his little toddler way, Andy hated me with as much voracity as I hated Mom. Did he wish to be anywhere in the world except there in that room with me? Did he want me dead, the way I wanted "her" dead?

I soon came to regret all the mornings I tortured Andy because of nothing more than his natural childhood tendencies.

The Lariscys called a family meeting, but this one wasn't a normal family meeting. The Lariscy kids and Andy were noticeably absent. Louie, Eric, and I joined Henry and Jerline around the dining room table. "We're so grateful you kids have come into our lives. Each one of you has brought us your very own special brand of joy. We want you to know that beyond the shadow of a doubt," Jerline began. She spoke slowly, as if to not let her thoughts get ahead of her speech.

My mind raced. What was she saying? This "family meeting" was reminiscent of the day we left the O'Donnells' house. *Here we go again*, I thought. *I may as well go start to pack right now.* Jerline's voice ushered me out of my head and back to the meeting around the table. She continued to explain that it would be a while before Dad could come and get us. The child welfare agency labored to find someone in the family willing to take us in, but after having made contact with all of the extended family, nobody was willing to take us.

By definition, foster care is meant to be a stopgap between emergency shelter and the ultimate reunion between the children and their family. *Okay, so we stay here*, I thought.

I was totally fine with the possibility that we would stay with the Lariscys forever. There were certainly worse places to be.

Henry and Jerline continued. They explained that Aunt Mary was willing to adopt Andy because he was still so young, and since he wasn't Dad's son, it made more sense that Aunt Mary—Mom's sister—would raise him. *So that's it*, I thought. Andy was going to leave.

Flashbacks of Gayle and the pain of her absence immediately flooded my soul. That familiar pit in my stomach returned. Once again, I felt responsible for the loss of yet another sibling. He was going back to Ohio to be adopted by family and the rest of us were staying here. I wrestled with the struggle that I loved Andy and didn't want him to go, but he was a pain in the ass and had been primarily my responsibility since he was a baby. At the same time, I was jealous that he was being adopted and the rest of us weren't. And why? Because he was still a baby. And the cycle of betrayal continued; from Dad choosing Myra and her kids over us, Mom choosing the thug life over us, and now aunts and uncles choosing anything, anything at all over us.

Before our family meeting wrapped up, and while I was still contemplating Andy's impending departure, Jerline and Big Henry announced that they'd requested that Aunt Mary delay Andy's adoption so we could take a family vacation to their summer home in the Smoky Mountains. This was extra special because it would be our last summer with Andy.

Smoky Mountain Summer

Up until our entry into the foster system, quality family time was an alien concept. The Lariscys made sure to introduce us to a robust variety of family oriented activities. Taking full advantage of the year-round optimal weather, we spent the bulk of our time outdoors. This culture followed us during our summers in Tennessee. More often than not, we'd pack a picnic basket full of bologna sandwiches, potato chips, Twinkies, and thermoses of Kool-Aid and sweet tea and head to the river for the day. We'd swim, fish, skip stones in the river, anything and everything to burn energy.

We would spend a few weeks in the Lariscy summer home in Pigeon Forge, Tennessee. They had an unassuming home that sat in the valley of the Great Smoky Mountains. With steep mountains on either side of us, we didn't have the luxury of dawn and twilight; the sun was blocked by the mountains unless it was practically overhead. Every day, Louie and I were tasked with fetching water from the creek. Equipped with two pails each, we would trek to the creek for the family's water.

No running water also meant no indoor plumbing. When nature called, we had to trudge around the back of the house and slightly up an incline to a long gravel road which led to the outhouse. No big deal in the glare of the summer sun, but when the sun descended behind the mountains and darkness engulfed the valley, only the bravest of souls would make the hike without batting an eye. Right on cue, Randy sensed my apprehension and took great delight in warning of the perils that awaited us on our inevitable midnight run. On those nights when my bladder woke me with a sense of urgency I couldn't ignore, I would have no choice but to brave the hike to the outhouse.

Randy's exaggerated warnings repeated themselves on an endless loop in my head:

"This place has bears and they come down off the mountains at night looking for food."

"Be cautious of the bats. They fly around in the dark and if they get caught up and tangled in your hair, we'll have no choice but to shave your head."

"The spiders around here grow enormous and you'll get really sick if they bite you."

Armed with nothing more than a flashlight, I set out on the lonely path while crickets and cicadas serenaded me. I'd like to think I courageously faced my fears and intrepidly walked to the outhouse. But, in reality, I ran as fast as I could, barefoot, with my hands and arms covering my head. My imagination was plagued with my biggest fears: bears, bats, and spiders. I envisioned bears tearing me limb from limb, bats swooping down from the sky to nest in my long blond hair, and colossal spiders swinging down from tree limbs on their freshly spun webs out to get me.

I wondered if anyone would hear me if I screamed for help. Would I be too paralyzed with fear to even make a peep? At the time, it hadn't occurred to me that I had already survived Mom, who had the temperament of a bear—always on guard and ready to attack. I'd also faced the risk of shaving my head due to an infestation of lice. And I'd had a terrible spider bite that caused a raging infection, the scar from which I still had. I was stronger than I realized.

While the mountains harbored scary things, they also offered some treasures. Louie and I would take off up the mountain and spend all day picking blackberries and raspberries. Jerline would turn these little gems into compotes and jams, she would can them for later, she would add them to pancakes, muffins, anything she could think of. We never grew tired of these mouthwatering culinary creations that were beyond my wildest imagination. Smoky Mountain summers allowed for childhood innocence to be restored. We soaked up all the fun and carefree moments we possibly could. We were making up for lost time.

When we weren't fetching water, picking berries, or playing

in the swimming hole, we'd look for other adventures to keep us busy. There, on the side of the mountain, was a large, lumpy brown mud dauber nest. This wasn't an ordinary mud dauber nest that you might see hanging on the side of a garage or tool shed. This was the mother of all mud dauber nests. It was at least three feet long and nearly that wide too. Depending on how many mud daubers were involved in the construction, it probably took weeks to build. Its sheer size suggested the nest was the equivalent to a multi-family condominium.

Lil' Henry and Randy had taken off to go into town, Jerline was in the kitchen prepping one of her to-die-for blackberry creations, Big Henry was tinkering around the cabin, and Crystal was down for a nap. This left me and the boys to find something to do. I had picked a fistful of dandelions and was busy tying them into a daisy chain.

Louie, Eric, and Andy passed time by lobbing rocks at the enormous mud dauber nest that had intrigued them for a while. Each rock that made contact with the nest resulted in a little bit of the condo crumbling away. Bam! There went some of the nest. Whack! There went some more. I could hear occasional grunts escape the boys as they lobbed rock after rock at their ticking time-bomb of a target. They threw the rocks as if a scouting agent from a Major League Baseball team were there to recruit their next star pitcher.

Eventually, after an hour or so of the nonstop assault, enough of the structure had crumbled to the ground and out came a swarm of furious mud daubers. I know how I would feel if some out-of-town thugs destroyed my home and threatened my family, and I can only imagine the fury these mud daubers harbored against my brothers.

Hundreds of angry mud daubers unified together and zeroed in on the boys like a heat-seeking missile. Louie and Eric outran the swarm, but in true Darwinian fashion, the youngest and weakest of the trio could not escape the mud daubers' revenge. The irony is that three-year-old Andy lacked the strength to throw a rock the necessary distance and the hand-eye coordination to actually strike the nest. I'm certain that none of the rocks Andy threw ever made contact with the nest. Regardless, Andy was overcome by mud dauber stings.

Kids have a wide range of cries. The cranky *I need a nap* cry has a different tone than that of a *temper tantrum* cry one hears coming from the toy department at the local store. Worst of all is the *help me, I'm in pain* cry. These cries and more are universal, and every parent develops a keen sense to identify them immediately and act accordingly. When Big Henry heard Andy's frantic *help me I'm dying* cry, he sprang from the house like a shot from a gun. Like a true first responder hero who runs into a burning building when everyone else is running out, he jetted toward Andy. In one swift motion, Big Henry swiped his signature green-and-white ball cap from his head, scooped up Andy, and swatted away the mud daubers that were still on the attack. Andy's little body was already swollen and bright red, evidence of the mud daubers' rage, and I'm certain his three-year-old mind couldn't grasp why he felt like he was on fire.

Having completed his mission of rescuing Andy from the attack, but not sure what to do next, Big Henry carried Andy into the house and called out for Jerline. The puzzle pieces came together for Jerline in an instant: Andy's desperate and pain-fueled cries, the red welts on his body, and the words "mud daubers." Jerline took control of the situation with authority in her voice. She directed Big Henry to take Andy to the bath house and put him in the tub. At the same time, Louie and I were directed to make sure the water pails were full, and if not, to run to the creek to fill them. After Andy soaked in the tub of cool water to help soothe the venomous stings, he was wrapped in a towel and Big Henry carried him back into the house. Jerline finished the first-aid task by dabbing a salve on each of Andy's sting sites.

We had our share of down time. Evenings around a campfire toasting marshmallows and making s'mores became a cherished memory of my Smoky Mountain summers. When we had our fill of the campfire, Randy entertained himself by taking us snipe hunting. Off we'd go, deep into the woods in search of the elusive snipe. Chirp…chirp…tweet…chirp. "Did you hear that?" Randy would ask, indicating our close proximity to an unsuspecting snipe.

"I heard it! I heard it over here!" I would eagerly reply as I tiptoed along in the woods. I wanted desperately to make Randy proud of me as I caught my very first snipe that summer. Little did I know that I was on a fool's errand. Snipe hunting was something that adults invented to enjoy some peace and quiet while occupying restless and rowdy kids.

We also enjoyed the essential summer pastimes like catching fireflies and playing with June bugs. The June bugs were my personal favorite. They were at least an inch long and nearly as wide. Sporting green iridescent wings that folded over their backs when not in flight, the June bugs were fun to play with and pretty to watch. We learned that we could tie string around one of their legs and let them fly while we held on to the other end of the string. This created annoyed June bugs that would fly in circles like the rotors on helicopters as they tried to escape from us. We harbored no malice or ill will toward the creatures in our captivity; we just innocently played with them as children do.

River tubing and rafting were some of the best ways to spend a hot Tennessee afternoon. Nothing was better than leisurely floating down the Pigeon River on an inner tube. The sun was bright but not scorching; the air was lighter than the stagnant, heavy, hell's furnace air that Florida offered in the summer. There was a sweet, fresh smell in the air.

For more adventure, we would raft on the river. One time I was sharing a raft with Randy. This raft wasn't exactly river-worthy; it was more of a glorified pool toy, barely large enough for two people. There we were, enjoying a leisurely float down the Pigeon River, not a soul around to disturb our brother/sister outing.

Our chit-chatting and sight-seeing abruptly stopped when we noticed there was no more river on the horizon! We were past the point of no return. We had no option but to go over the falls and hope for the best. Randy, probably scared out of his mind, had to remain calm and prepare me for this impromptu adventure that could very well have ended very, very badly.

"Hold on! Just hold on with all your strength. Do not let go!" Randy demanded. The edgy tone of his voice indicated this was not a game like snipe hunting. I knew this was our only hope and I trusted Randy.

I was scared and white-knuckling it the whole way. If Randy was scared, he didn't show it. As we approached the falls, I gripped the raft's handle with everything I had in me. I watched as the water toiled more and more and the gentle sounds of water lapping around the raft were replaced by a dull roar that was growing increasingly fierce. *So this is what white water rafting is*, I thought. But we weren't equipped for white-water rafting. Neither of us had life jackets or helmets for safety.

1…2…3…ready or not, here we gooooo, and we were on our way over. I sucked in a lungful of air just as we crested the top of the falls. I kept telling myself to not let go of the raft handle, even if that meant I died holding on to it.

We were in free fall. It felt like my stomach was in my

throat and I squeezed my eyes shut tightly. We splashed down, then were immediately submerged. Water from the falls pounded us beneath the surface.

I soon popped up nearby. The raft's buoyancy and my death grip on its handle were what led me to the water's surface. I looked around and could not find Randy. *Where is he*, I wondered. I scanned the area as I caught my breath. In what seemed like an eternity, but was really more like a few moments later, Randy surfaced downstream. Not only did the force of the waterfall push him below the surface, but the river's swift current carried him away.

Randy swam to the riverbank and climbed out, and then he ran back upstream to where I had made my way to the bank and was climbing out. Only then, when we looked back at the falls, did we realize just how big the drop was. "Oh my God! Look at that! That has to be at least a nine-foot drop!" Randy exclaimed. "If you had let go of that raft, you wouldn't have survived!" Randy was relieved that I was okay, and the look on his face said it all: I had once again cheated death.

While there was never a dull moment with the family in Pigeon Forge, I still liked to get out on my own and find adventures. Regina was a few years older than me, but we enjoyed each other's company. I met Regina at the local church when Jerline sent us kids down the road to service one evening. It was a regular church service, but a lot of the kids hung out in the back.

Not recognizing us as locals, Regina walked up and introduced herself. We clicked immediately. "I live right there," she said as she pointed catty-corner from the church property. "Come over tomorrow and we'll hang out."

I was excited to have met a new friend. She was literally the only other kid in the immediate area in one of the only houses around. I spent much of my summer with her. On Sunday mornings, I would walk a mile or so barefoot on the one-lane gravel road to her house and we'd go to church together.

Regina shared my enthusiasm for music, and we'd spend hours in her room listening to the radio and her collection of cassette tapes; she introduced me to the music of Prince and Heart.

The heavenly smell of fresh-baked chocolate chip cookies would waft from the kitchen and into her room, and if we didn't tear ourselves away from the music, Regina's mom would pop in with a plate of cookies for us.

It takes a certain skill, one that requires patience and cat-like reflexes, to be able to record a song from the radio, but by the end of the summer, both of us were quite adept at it. Regina and I would long-sufferingly sit by the radio and wait for a favorite song to come on, and then craftily record it on a blank cassette, old-school style. By the time we left Tennessee, I had quite a nice collection of pirated songs. The hours Regina and I spent listening to the radio and harvesting songs for our mix tapes were all but a rite of passage for anyone growing up in the '80s. We'd dance to the fun songs, talk and giggle through the commercials, and imitate the over-the-top disc jockeys who punctuated music marathons with occasional mandatory station identifications, weather and traffic reports, and information about local events.

One such interruption captured my attention. It was a trivia question with the opportunity to win a family dinner at a local restaurant. In addition to correctly answering the question, the winner had to be lucky caller number ten. *I've got nothing to lose,* I thought. The odds were against me, but that had never stopped me before. "Seven states call this their official state bird. What is it?" The DJ dramatically asked the trivia question.

My mind raced through all the birds in the avian world. Robin, sparrow, hummingbird, flamingo—the list went on—but when I came to the stately cardinal and pictured it in my mind, I was certain this fine bird was a popular state bird. I frantically dialed the radio station, hopeful that I was lucky number ten. I really wanted to win dinner for my family. The Lariscys took in four needy kids; we had nothing but each other, painful memories, and hopes and dreams. They nurtured and taught us, met our physical and emotional needs, fed us literally and spiritually, not for the chance to win a big luxurious home or an exotic vacation, but simply because there was a need. I would love to be able to pay back just a small fraction of what they'd done for me and my brothers—to show my gratitude and contribute in a small way to this family who sheltered and loved us.

My daydreaming came to an abrupt end when the DJ answered the phone with a booming "Congratulations! You're caller number ten. Which bird do seven states call their official state bird?"

"The cardinal," I answered.

I couldn't believe my luck. I was caller number ten and I was on the radio. My voice was being broadcast over the air just like Prince's "Purple Rain" and Culture Club's "Karma Chameleon." The DJ confirmed that I was correct. Best day ever! I squealed with delight as the DJ announced to the Pigeon Forge listeners that I had just won dinner for my family at Duff's Smorgasbord in nearby Gatlinburg, Tennessee.

That night at dinner, I was so proud that I could barely eat. I looked around the table at everyone eating, talking, and laughing, and I was elated that I had made this happen. I was able to give back to the family who meant so much to me. The smorgasbord offered so many fine dinner choices, and by definition, it was all you could eat. We ate our fill of fried chicken, roast beef, chicken and noodles, and endless sides. It truly is better to give than to receive.

Going to Silver Dollar City, the precursor to Dollywood, was a highlight of the summer. They had all the standard amusement park trappings: rides and roller coasters, forbidden food, music and shows—you name it, Silver Dollar City had it. The Lariscys planned our day at the amusement park as the crown jewel of an already fun-filled summer in Pigeon Forge. The boys had each other for macho bonding, but Jerline was cognizant of my need for sisterly companionship, so she allowed me to invite Regina to join us. I looked forward to the opportunity to have my friend along for the day. On the morning of our big day at Silver Dollar City, all of us kids piled in the back of the family truck. We were packed like sardines, but it was a relatively short ride off the mountain and into town.

The Coal Miner Ride was tame and featured animatronic coal miners that talked to us as we passed by in little boats. The Log Lagoon was not tame; its sole purpose was to thrill and soak. Ride engineers used the area's topography for the ride's spirit—the Log Lagoon was built into the side of the mountain. This was the most refreshing and exhilarating ride in the summer heat. Soaked clothes were our badges of honor—they meant we had the guts to ride down the Great Smoky Mountains and splash the afternoon away, and we felt an immediate kinship to anyone we saw in drenched clothes.

Onward we walked through the thoroughfare, taking away fond memories and leaving nothing but wet footprints in our wake and not a care in the world other than what fun we would find around the next corner. Through the symphony of summertime bliss, I heard music. "Rocky Top" was the song, but I was only vaguely familiar with it. The rhythm found my soul and nested there. It was infectious, and I just couldn't be still.

With my guidance, or maybe it was more insistence, we found our way to the grandstand and settled in for some good old-fashioned, Southern country entertainment. The performers on the stage were cloggers—the men were in jeans, cowboy shirts, cowboy hats, and the obligatory cowboy boots. The women wore traditional clogging dresses similar in style to square dance dresses. Metal taps loosely affixed to the bottoms of their boots and shoes made a jingling sound when they'd kick their feet and a clanging sound when stepped. Reminiscent of the cancan, the women swished the ruffles of their skirts to accentuate their movements. I was mesmerized.

Finally, at ten years old, I was actually happy. Summer was winding down, and we had to pack up everything and head back to Florida. My Smoky Mountain summer taught me much about life. I learned that superheroes don't always wear capes; sometimes they wear green-and-white ball caps. I learned that you can hunt for invented pests and find total bliss. I learned how to relate to my peers and not be their victim. I learned that no matter how grand a gift you give away, your soul is rewarded with even grander gifts. My Smoky Mountain summer was everything I could have wished for, but I didn't even know that I wanted or needed. That summer was a dream come true and has been a benchmark by which I measure other summer vacations.

Smoky Mountains, Pigeon Forge, TN

Randy circa age 13

*Regina, 13
years old*

*The Cabin on Mill Creek
in Pigeon Forge*

Temporary Fix

Not too long after returning from Tennessee, we packed up all of Andy's belongings, and Big Henry and Jerline left with him. They took Andy to Ohio where Aunt Mary was waiting to finalize his adoption. I felt a sense of relief that he would be going to a good home and I wouldn't need to mother him, but this liberation was overshadowed by the same nagging guilt that haunted me during the aftermath of Gayle's unexpected departure. The goodbye was sad, but the finality of it didn't really hit me right away. During this new period of transition, Lil' Henry and Randy were tasked with being the unofficial guardians of my sanity. By not making a big deal out of it, they proved that life would go on, and I would just have to learn to cope with the emptiness that remained in Andy's wake. When I didn't bounce back as quickly as they'd hoped, they searched for a distraction—something to otherwise interrupt my internal conflict. Their solution? A scary…no, a terrifying movie.

The universal problem with big brothers, whether they are biological, half-brothers, stepbrothers, or foster brothers, is that they love to torture the younger kids in the family. Moreover, the younger kids idolize their older siblings so much that they allow, even at times encourage, this quasi-mistreatment just for the opportunity to spend more time with them. It was rare that the Lariscys left us in the care of their two sons.

In their defense, Lil' Henry and Randy struggled with the morality of their decision to allow me to watch *The Exorcist* with them, but I assured them that I could handle it. "No, you're only ten. Maybe you should just go to bed like Eric," they said.

Then it became more of a challenge for me to prove them wrong. "Dammit, I can do anything a boy can do," I told them. "Let me stay up and watch it and I'll prove it to you," I negotiated.

Once Eric was in bed, we made a big bowl of popcorn and took it into the TV room. This alone was taboo; Jerline had a strict rule that food was only allowed in the kitchen and dining room. With a devil-may-care attitude, we turned off all the lights in the house, Randy put the tape in the VCR, then flung himself on the reclining chair while Lil' Henry stretched out on the couch. Louie and I were parked on the floor nearby.

We were all within arm's reach of the popcorn, but once the movie started, I was transfixed. Forgetting all about the popcorn was nothing. I forgot to blink, and at times I forgot to breathe, but I needed to prove myself to Lil' Henry and Randy, so I willed myself the fortitude to watch. *The Exorcist* had me spellbound as Regan's bed levitated and violently shook. Every hair on my body stood at attention as Regan's head spun around.

With all of my senses heightened, I could feel Lil' Henry and Randy's occasional gaze as they monitored my reaction and state of well-being. They wanted to make sure I was: 1) still watching and not covering my eyes, and 2) not totally flipping out on them. Part of the deal I negotiated with them was that I'd never tell Big Henry and Jerline that they let me watch the movie in the first place. If I was freaking out, I'd surely not be able to keep this secret.

In actuality, I was afraid to look away. I rationalized that if I concentrated hard enough on the movie, then the demon would stay there and not come into the house. I could feel my heart pounding in my extremities, and when I swallowed, it was in large gulps.

I didn't dare move a muscle during the entire movie. *The Exorcist* had me terrified all the way to the end. I wish I could say that I felt better once the movie ended, but the fact was, that's when the real terror started. Every little sound I heard was a demon coming to get me. I even "heard" sounds that weren't there. I saw the white-faced demon every time I closed my eyes to sleep. I was too afraid to get up in the middle of the night to go to the bathroom, certain that I would feel the death grip of the demon grab my legs and drag me to hell. I felt Andy's absence in the worst way. Even though he was just a toddler, his presence would have been enough to keep the demon at bay. Now that I was all alone in that room, I was vulnerable to the demon's torture—torture that I felt I deserved to balance my sins against Andy.

I remember the feeling of holding a full bladder in Tennessee in the wee hours of the morning to avoid the real but exaggerated threat of bats, bears, and spiders, but this was an imaginary, albeit heightened, fear of things that go bump in the night. So instead, I would try to hold it until morning and often ended up wetting the bed. When that happened, I would contort myself around the wet spot to find a dry area and fall back asleep until morning. Then I would get up early and throw my sheets in the washer so no one would know what I did. Even though I was terrified by *The Exorcist*, it did the trick; I was able to get through the worst part of Andy leaving. Big brothers are not so bad.

In the days and weeks since Andy had left, random memories invaded my consciousness: caring for Andy as an infant in the back of the bar, feeding him bread and sugar to fill his belly, watching his baby teeth come in black, helping him learn to blow bubbles in the O'Donnells' pool, losing my temper when he trashed our bedroom, and coming to his defense when Jerline yelled at him. I don't remember my outward reaction at Andy's absence, but Jerline must have picked up on some level of depression because she and I spent a weekend transforming the room I shared with Andy into a pink Strawberry Shortcake-themed room that suited me just fine.

It wasn't long before school started and routines settled in. Each day after school, Louie, Eric, and I would go to the Boys and Girls Club until Jerline finished her school bus route and came to pick us up. Designed like a micro campus, the Boys and Girls Club had an administration building, two activity buildings, picnic tables, and an open lawn area. The club afforded us a chance to interact with other kids our age and become involved with various activities.

To get out of the Florida heat, we'd hang out in the rec room that had a couple of pinball machines, a Skee-Ball game, and two pool tables. There was also a lake on the property where we could splash around, swim, and race for bragging rights. In addition to swimming, the club alternated various structured activities throughout the week: soccer, baseball, water ballet, and arts and crafts.

My activities of choice were water ballet and the clogging team. I've always loved the water, and being in water was a natural choice for me. More important than that was the opportunity to take clogging classes and be on the clogging team. This was really special because it was an extra-curricular activity and the cloggers had to stay late for class two nights a week. The additional expense that the Lariscys paid for me to attend was a true gift. Among my many lessons from the clogging team, I learned how to be a team player—we all succeeded or failed as one. I also learned about choreography and costumes. Moreover, I learned self-confidence as I performed on stage in front of an audience. Before this, my only other experience in front of a group of people was when I was set aside as an outcast in my class for having head lice.

Yes, Andy had left, and I was feeling the full impact of this, but true to the Lariscy way, they rallied behind me, the one who felt his absence the most. In their own individual perfect ways, each of them got me through. I learned that life moves on and we can either wallow in our misery or move on with our lives. I only hoped that Andy was acclimating to Aunt Mary and his new life.

Jerline, Andy, and Henry Lariscy Sr. in 1984
on the day that Andy was adopted by Aunt Mary

Royal Transformation

The Southern states are the unofficial hub of beauty pageants, and since Jerline had insisted the state pay for the surgery to correct my crossed eyes, I was now pageant ready—or at least ready enough to be transformed. Being the pageant mom that she was, Jerline couldn't resist entering me into my first pageant, Little Miss Turkey Creek. By this time, Jerline had entered Crystal into every available pageant, and Crystal had amassed enough trophies to nearly rival an Olympic athlete. In my mind, this more than qualified Jerline as an expert, and I submitted to her tutelage. She coached me on standing tall, walking like a lady, poise, and pivoting, all while smiling until my face hurt. For all the scrutiny and criticism beauty pageants get, they really can be a useful resource in helping to mold a young girl into a lady, and most importantly, if correctly implemented, teaching the virtues of congeniality and humility.

One foot in front of the other, back straight, head high, arms flared at the elbows; Jerline would coach as I mastered the one voluntary skill I've known since I was about a year old. Her Southern charm made these daily drills more palatable even though it felt like I was in boot camp.

The next big challenge was to find a pageant dress. Not willing to pay full retail price, which could easily exceed $300 in 1983, we hit the local garage sale circuit. If you're patient and persistent, you can find a diamond in the rough, and that's exactly what we did. Jerline found a beautiful dress with layers and layers of white ruffles. My new dress was that wonderful shade between baby blue and royal blue, and it had so many ruffles that the skirt flared out like a bell, especially when I added the crinoline slip. Modesty was still in fashion, and I distinctly remember that this dress was knee-length. The ensemble was finished off with a pair of white anklet socks that folded down to show a lacy ruffle, white patent leather shoes, and clip-on earrings. I had come a long way since the days of playing in a trash dumpster, and I was proud of the young lady I was becoming. For the first time, I could see a future beyond tomorrow or next week. I could feel my life beginning to take root, and I very much liked what I saw.

By the day of the pageant, all of the deep preparation was done. It was time to put the shine on. Lil' Henry's girlfriend, Jeanie, came over and painted my nails while Jerline and her mom, Virginia, worked on my hair and makeup. I felt like a princess being doted on by her ladies-in-waiting.

The fumes of the nail polish and hairspray, the mascara, a little bit of blush to enhance my youthful beauty, all the attention—everyone was in my personal space getting me ready. I could feel beads of perspiration forming on my forehead and the nape of my neck. *Ba-boom, ba-boom, ba-boom*, my heart was pounding in my chest, the room began to spin, voices sounded a hundred miles away, and then boom, I was out. When I came to, I was lying on the floor and three concerned faces were staring down at me. Someone had propped my feet up on a chair and someone else had splashed cold water on my face. Jerline attributed my fainting spell to the fact that I hadn't eaten, so she fixed me a snack, but I was too nervous to eat. The reality of what I was about to do struck me like a freight train.

We eventually arrived at the pageant, which was being held in the ballroom of a local hotel. The place was crawling with many hopeful little girls—some were more hopeful than others—and an equal number of anxious pageant moms mindlessly popping their gum to release nervous energy.

Peppered throughout the general seating area and milling around in adjacent hallways were dads and siblings, many of whom seemed to wish they were someplace else. I recognized a few faces from school and even one contestant from a different time and place. It was Tiffany, the over-indulged spoiled brat from school when we lived in the trailer park in Plant City. This was the girl who ruthlessly tormented me for having to sit apart from the rest of the class when I had head lice. She was cruel to anyone who could not offer her an advantage in the social warfare of grade school. She would mock and ridicule me, or if I was lucky, she would just ignore me.

The beauty of my metamorphosis was that I was completely unrecognizable to her. Never in her wildest dreams could I have focused eyes, shiny and clean bouncy hair, beautiful clothes that fit properly, and an air of confidence that rivaled that of royalty. The sad truth was that she was sickeningly sweet to me, assuming I was her genuine competition and not the scourge of the Earth as she had treated me before. My already nervous stomach tightened as Tiffany approached me. I was prepared for her taunts as she berated me for ever thinking I could win a beauty pageant. "Aww, your dress is so pretty," she said as she admired my outfit, my hairdo, my whole ensemble. At that moment, my mind raced through several belittling responses, and then a barrage of insults came to mind. Like a supercomputer my mind calculated one response after another, each custom-designed to hurt and insult her.

Instead of revealing my identity, I swallowed my bitterness and simply said, "Thank you. Yours is nice, too." I decided that since I was dressed like a proper lady, I'd behave like one too. Plus, I didn't want to disgrace Jerline and the proper upbringing she had been providing.

A potpourri of hairspray hung heavy in the ladies' room as the pageant moms touched up and teased already overdone hair—it was the '80s, after all. Soon, my age class, ten to fourteen, was instructed to assemble off-stage. It was finally our turn. One by one, each contestant paraded across the stage in that now-familiar pageant walk that I had mastered. *Here goes nothing*, I thought as I approached the stage for my fateful walk. Heel, toe, heel, toe, I gracefully placed one foot in front of the other just as Jerline had drilled into me. I could hear her voice on a repeating loop in my head: back straight, shoulders back, head up, arms flared at the elbows, eye contact with the judges, and smile, always smile.

I made my way to the announcer who asked me one of the obligatory pageant questions. "If you had one million dollars, what would you do with it?"

A million dollars? That's my question? Really? Did he have any idea of my background? I would have been happy with fifty dollars. After a moment of careful consideration, I replied, "I would like to take my mom (I referred to Jerline as Mom) to London. I hear it's a beautiful city, and I think she would like it there."

I heard a collective *aww* from the audience. As I scanned the crowd of pageant moms and dads, I looked to Jerline for the only thing I needed at that moment—her reassurance that I had answered well. Her enormous smile was all the confirmation I needed. And just like that, my turn was over. I made my way off the stage and toward Jerline as the pageant continued and the judging commenced. Of course, she was sitting in the middle of the row, and I remember climbing over pageant moms, dads, and siblings, stepping over purses and duffel bags as gracefully as I could. I reminded myself of Bugs Bunny as I passed each person, saying excuse me, pardon me, pardon me, excuse me, I'm sorry, et cetera. I was fully aware that my puffy pageant dress was swatting them in their faces. By now, my earlobes were throbbing from the clip-on earrings, the dress was becoming itchy, and my feet hurt.

Meanwhile, up on stage, the announcer was congratulating all the girls in my age class for a wonderful effort. She went on to declare the runners-up and then the winner.

As I approached Jerline, she gave me a maternal reassuring nod accompanied by her warm smile. "Michelle, honey, you did great!" She beamed. Pride replaced my bone marrow; I simply lived to hear those words. I was on a natural high, even though I knew I didn't stand a chance of winning against these beauty pageant veterans.

As soon as I sat down next to Jerline, satisfied in the effort I put into my very first pageant, she started patting my back and nudging my arm. "Michelle! Honey! Get up there, they called your number, sweetie! You won!"

Climbing over all those people again didn't seem like such a burden as I made my way back up to the stage. I almost floated up there, elated that I had won my first pageant. There was a flurry of activity around me. Someone draped the Little Miss Turkey Creek sash on me, someone else handed me a large bouquet of flowers which I instinctively cradled like a swaddled baby, and then came the crown. *I've made it! I've transformed from dumpster to doll!*

This crown was fit for a queen—which was how I felt. It was a gold-plated semi-circle crown with combs in the back to help secure it to my head. The crown was rimmed with ornate peaks that stretched increasingly taller as they approached the front. Each peak provided a dwelling for a dangling onyx gem. I was struck by the weight of the crown; it felt like it could have weighed twenty pounds, but I'm sure it was more like two.

There I stood, the 1983 Little Miss Turkey Creek, bouquet of flowers in one arm, waving to the crowd with the other. I can't be sure, but I think all of my pageant prep work flew out the window, and my wave looked more like that of the ten-year-old kid I felt like on the inside and not the princess that I looked like on the outside. I looked over at the runners-up and saw Tiffany crying tears of defeat, failure, and second best. I was crying too, but my tears were from happiness, elation, and pride.

Jerline didn't seem to mind that my tears were ruining my makeup. She knew this win was much more than a sash, flowers, and a crown. It was the victory I needed to prove that I was more than my past. It was the beginning of what launched me into self-awareness, self-approval, and self-respect.

Now that the pageant was over, it was time to fulfill my Little Miss Turkey Creek duties. There was a parade in Plant City, and I needed to be there. The whole process of hair and makeup had to be repeated, so Jerline, Virginia, and Jeanie worked to recreate what they had done a few weeks earlier. It was time once again for a curling iron, mousse, and hairspray for my blond locks, and mascara, blush, and lipstick for my face.

At the same time, Lil' Henry was outside washing and waxing his new Camaro convertible. I'm not sure if Lil' Henry was volunteering to use his pageant-winning little foster-sister to show off his shiny new Camaro, or use his shiny new Camaro to show off his pageant-winning little foster-sister. I'd like to think it was the latter. With the top down, Lil' Henry put a blanket on the back of the convertible for me to sit on, and he drove the parade route with Jeanie by his side. The car was adorned with streamers and a poster on each side that announced my name and which pageant I was representing.

My job as a pageant queen was to simply wave and toss candy into the crowd. Like a queen tossing gold coins at the feet of her subjects, I felt like royalty as cheers and applause erupted at each new passing vehicle. I waved to my adoring public, my people, as I lobbed handfuls of candy that children eagerly reached for. Through the din of the crowd I heard "Michelle, Michelle! Over here, throw some candy over here!"

I looked to see who was calling me by name. It was Becky and Charlie. They looked like the same wild, unkempt, unsupervised heathens I remembered. They were part of the mutant-brained demon spawn from the trailer park. They had nothing but disdain for me then, and now they were carrying on like we were long-lost friends. In an instant, my mind ran through a multitude of sequences; I recalled the frantic terror they instilled as they persecuted me and rallied other kids to do the same. The hurtful names that inflicted harm far more sinister than the physical damage they caused. Even though Cock-Eyed Pissy Pants got her eyes fixed, cleaned up, and put on makeup and a dress, still, in some tiny way that haunts me on my darkest nights, I still sometimes feel like that pitiable little girl. That's the scourge of bullying.

My initial thought was to calculate distance, velocity, and trajectory. I wanted to hurl the candy so hard that it would hit them and hurt them the way they hurt me with rocks and clumps of dried mud. All of a sudden, without warning or consciously doing so, I looked at Becky and Charlie and saw them through a different lens. It was a lens of maturity, a lens of compassion and empathy, and perhaps a dose of pity as well. I had the benefit of a nurturing and caring family where they didn't. Not only that, but I was also blessed with the grace to absorb what was bestowed upon me and reflect the blessings back to the world. Then, as if Jiminy Cricket himself were sitting on my shoulder, the voice of reason demanded that I rise above the pettiness and act like a young lady who would honor Jerline.

At that moment, I appreciated that I was in a much better place than Becky and Charlie. I escaped the oppression and squalor of that trailer park, and they were still stuck there. I didn't need to act the way they had acted toward me only a couple years earlier; I was able to rise above it.

I continued with the pageant circuit for a while and earned

runner-up a few times, but never again got crowned Little Miss anything, and I was fine with this. I believe I gleaned what lessons I needed from my experiences in pageants, lessons I would carry with me. I wasn't born into the pageant life, and I was able to walk away from it just as easily as I walked into it. Jerline was equally satisfied with the impact that being crowned Little Miss Turkey Creek had on me. It wasn't about the road to Miss America, it never was. It was about proving to myself that I was somebody, and that I have poise, grace, maturity, and empathy.

My very first pageant,
Little Miss Turkey Creek,
10 years old

Jeanie and Lil' Henry circa
1984–1985

Me wearing my
crown the day of
the parade

The Ah-ha Moment

Life went on. I was getting used to Andy's absence, but I often wondered how he was doing and if he missed us. We were his whole world for his first three years. He undoubtedly had a significant adjustment period. But once he was gone, he was gone. We didn't get updates on his well-being or calls from Aunt Mary to check on us.

I started sixth grade and my eleventh birthday rolled around. I was allowed to invite a couple girls from school to help me celebrate. We had dinner and cake with ice cream—nothing fancy, but it was my special day. Jerline handed me a gift box wrapped up with a pretty bow. I enthusiastically unwrapped the box, trying to do so with a cool maturity that I did not yet possess. I squealed with delight as I opened my very first makeup kit. Oohs and ahs escaped my lips as I studied all the pretty colors of blush, eye shadow, and lip gloss. I was finally permitted to wear makeup and not just for pageants.

Budget restraints, environmental consciousness, whatever the reason, we had to share our school bus with another school in the district. This posed no problem for me, as I've always enjoyed being around people, and an extra stop or two didn't cause any consternation. I remember the cutest boy boarding the bus and looking for a seat. He had blond hair, blue eyes, and an adorable dimple in each cheek. He was a junior Adonis. I always noticed him because I thought he was the cutest boy I had ever seen. When he sat near me, I would steal glances as much as possible without being caught. He once sat with me, and over the din of after-school chatter and the rumble of the diesel bus, we struck up a modest conversation. We learned each other's names, grades, and the very basic information one solicits as prepubescents just mastering the skill of meeting new friends.

As we trudged through the school year, it became evident that we had a mutual fondness. I began to notice that although the bus would be fairly full, there were still seats left to share, but Billy would make a beeline to me and plop down. Soon I would try to save a spot for Billy, but if someone else approached needing a seat, I would never deny them. Once I got home from school, I would go out back to check on Bessie and Betsy, then grab a snack and sit down to tackle my homework.

My ah-ha moment came one afternoon when my

concentration was broken as I heard Jerline call my name from the kitchen. "Michelle—honey, the phone is for you."

I didn't even hear it ring, I thought as I fashioned a make-shift bookmark by closing my pencil in the book. Jerline handed the phone receiver to me and returned to preparing dinner.

"Hello?" I said, expecting it to be Ericka or one of my other friends from school, probably calling to check which vocabulary words to study or which math problems were assigned. Without caller ID, the suspense of learning who was on the other end of the line climbed to a fever pitch until the moment you heard the disembodied voice, and sometimes, if it wasn't who you were expecting, the suspense continued until the introduction.

"Hi Michelle, it's Billy." Billy, the super cute boy from the school bus was calling me. Oh, this was serious. I needed ultra-privacy. I stretched the cord from the gold rotary phone that was mounted to the kitchen wall into the pantry and shut the door. Standing in the tiny space with canned goods, I twisted the cord around my finger as Billy and I spoke. I hoped my schoolgirl delight was somewhat tempered, and that I didn't sound like a complete idiot. Billy asked if I would be his girlfriend and hold his hand on the bus.

What?! Are you kidding me?! My mind raced. My very first boyfriend. "Yes!" I exclaimed with boundless fervor. We ended our conversation, and I opened the pantry door to find Jerline, Lil' Henry, Randy, and Louie huddled right there.

With a smile and a wink, Jerline gave me a knowing look. She was happy for me and excited to usher me into this new phase of life. The boys, equally knowing, made kissing sounds and began the ageless ritual chant: "Michelle and Billy sitting in a tree, K-I-S-S-I-N-G…" As for me, I was flooded with emotion. Billy was the first boy who showed an interest in me, the whole me. I was more than the sum of my parts that just existed for others' enjoyment or amusement. Billy wasn't reacting to the pageant me with a fancy dress, hair, and makeup. It was the everyday before-and-after-school me that he liked. He saw the before-a-test me, the nervous-to-give-a-book-report me, the me when I had a cold, and the me in random moods, and he liked *me*. I didn't have to put on a false smile or pretend everything was peachy. In that moment, my ah-ha moment, I felt special, and pretty, and worthy. I felt like I could move a mountain.

5th grade picture, 10 years old

The Good Fight

Besides Billy, my best friend in the sixth grade was Ericka. She was an African-American girl and wore her hair in long ringlet spirals. I've always prided myself on not seeing the color of people's skin. Instead, I notice their hearts and souls. That's all that really matters to me. If you're a good person, that's the end of the story.

The same thing goes for unsavory people. This philosophy played out one day in school when a boy who disagreed with something Ericka said called her a dumb nigger. I glanced at Ericka to gauge her reaction. She held her head high as if she were employing techniques that her parents taught her for when she was confronted by racists, but her eyes told another story. Her eyes were filling with tears—yes, words really do hurt. As if a movie reel played before my eyes, I pictured each of the handful of people I'd ever heard mutter the N-word. Nothing conveys hate and ignorance more than that intolerable word.

Reflexes took over, and I sprang out of my seat so fast and with such velocity that I slid on my belly all the way across the huge round table we shared. Without giving it a second thought, I went all Louisville Slugger (minus the bat) on that despicable kid. "You dumbass white trash piece of shit!" I shouted as I slid across the table. I was louder than I intended, but I was so angry and he needed to feel my wrath. My arm was locked straight and my fist was clenched. I imagine I looked like Superman in flight. My fist found its intended target—that boy's nose.

The impact felt like a wrecking ball striking a little rubber ball. He immediately began to wail as blood ran down his face and soaked the front of his shirt. There I was, eye to eye with this racist menace, when my teacher's hand swooped down, grabbed my arm, and yanked me off the table. I laughed with satisfaction at the fact that he was crying—I had hopefully inflicted more damage to him than Ericka had sustained. It all happened so fast that it felt like a dream.

For the first time in my life, I was sent directly to the principal's office. I sat on the bench outside his office for what seemed like hours. I was pretty sure I wasn't going to be bestowed with a humanitarian award for single-handedly fighting racism, but I wasn't completely certain what was going to happen. A lecture, suspension, expulsion, firing squad—my mind went wild thinking of all the possibilities.

After a few minutes of waiting on the long wooden bench in the outer office, I was summoned in. The office was rather ordinary. There was a bookshelf or two full of books, not the suspected jars of students' tears. A few plaques and framed pictures hung on the walls, pictures of previous school events like the last day of school award ceremony, and a teacher banquet that included the superintendent. The principal's desk had a blotter stained by coffee rings where he scribbled notes and phone numbers. There was a framed photo of his family and a few paperclips tossed in a handmade ashtray that looked like one of his kids had made it in school. Off to the side, I saw the clunky microphone he used each morning to deliver the school announcements.

The principal sternly reviewed my misconduct and informed me that I was going to get three swats with the paddle, which was prominently hanging on the wall. As he reached for the paddle, he directed me to turn around, put my hands on the desk, and bend over. I was generally a good kid, and I'd never been subject to such punishment at school. As I assumed the position, I didn't look at the paddle; I didn't want to see it. I just wanted to get this over with.

SWAT! The first blow hit me like a ton of bricks. The pain gripped me, and I immediately cried. Pain radiated from the strike zone up my spine to my head and eyeballs. In comparison, the next two blows were lighter, but I'm not sure if I was in shock and therefore lost sensation, or if the principal realized his strength was no match for an eleven-year-old girl and lightened up a bit.   When he finished, he turned me around and asked if I knew why I got paddled. Through subsiding sobs, I answered, "Because that boy called my friend the 'N-word.'" He corrected me, and said it was because I hit that boy, and violence is never justified. I said I would do it again if I ever heard anyone insult any of my friends like that, and I asked why he wasn't sent in for a paddling, too. The principal said that he would be disciplined accordingly, made me promise not to hit, and sent me back to class.

Refusing to give anyone the satisfaction of knowing that I had been paddled or disciplined in any way, I pulled myself together and returned to class with my head held high. A hush fell over the classroom as I entered. Everyone was looking at me for any sign of what had transpired with the principal. As far as anyone knew, I did receive a humanitarian award for defending civility and fighting racist bigots.

The Christmas Gift

Throughout it all, as I endured the monsters at the trailer park, toxic spiders, a venomous mother, and mutant kids ranging from bullies to rapists, survived the midnight raid of our rescue, underwent lice and ringworm treatment at the children's home, enjoyed my own bedroom, my own clothes, a private swimming pool at the O'Donnells' house, summers in Tennessee, corrective eye surgery, beauty pageants, my first boyfriend at the Lariscys—I had no idea that back in Pennsylvania, Mr. Williams, the attorney, was keeping tabs on me. Somehow he tracked me down as the case regarding the drunk driver was still pending.

Mr. Williams connected with the Lariscys, and plans were made for me to visit him in Philadelphia accompanied by Jerline and Crystal. The weeks between finalizing the plans and traveling seemed to drag on forever. Every time I looked up and saw an airplane in the sky, I would get excited all over again—that would be me soon. But I just couldn't visualize myself on a plane. *Flying is for rich people*, I thought. It was nearly Christmas when I boarded the airplane for my very first flight. I was excited and nervous at the same time.

We soon landed in Philadelphia, and Mr. Williams met us at the airport in his mint green Mercedes. He was very tall and had a relentlessly serious look, which I found quite intimidating. I didn't come to understand his true care and concern for me until my adult years.

Mr. Williams got us settled in a swanky hotel; we were a few floors up and had a great view of the city. Jerline's endless remarks about how fancy it was helped me reflect on the stark contrast of my life just a few short years earlier. I was a child who played in a trash dumpster, a child left for dead by a miserable drunk driver, a child who watched her mom shoot up and then was abandoned by her with barely a food supply.

Now I was a guest in a posh hotel. The soap in the bathroom was wrapped like candy, and hotel employees held doors open for me and carried my bag for me. Someone made my bed every morning for me. There was such a gulf between my two realities, and I had difficulty coming to terms that *both* were *my* reality.

Mr. Williams drove us to the hospital where I treated after the accident. I had several doctor appointments as a condition of the still-pending court case. I was evaluated for any lasting effects from the accident—strength, flexibility, cognition and memory, vision, kidney function, the works. I'd already experienced a lifetime's worth of doctors, but I endured the poking and prodding because I knew that somehow it was important and necessary for the lawsuit.

After all of the medical stuff was done, Mr. Williams took me to see many of the nurses who had a hand in my care. Even though numerous nurses and aides helped me, I really only remembered Faye, the nurse who managed my recovery. The elevator doors opened, and just like magic I was transported back to December 1981; the stark hospital walls, the smell of antiseptic, the distant sound of machines and monitors beeping.

I couldn't help but flash back to the memories of countless walks down this very same corridor with Faye by my side as I learned to walk again. Moving at a pace that rivaled that of a glacial crawl, I depended on a walker to steady and support me. Faye was always by my side to cheer me on to that next painful step, and the next. She was my nurse, physical therapist, cheerleader, mother, and friend, all rolled into one heaven-sent being. As the memory waned, there I was, awkwardly standing in the hospital corridor with Jerline, Crystal, and Mr. Williams while the nursing staff gathered around me and marveled at my recovery. They rarely got to see their patients all recovered and healthy again.

A familiar voice drew my attention away from the impromptu reunion. "There's my beautiful girl." That voice could only belong to the angel who had tenderly cared for me in my darkest days. I could never forget that voice. I looked down the corridor and saw Faye. My Faye. She had emerged from a patient's room, and in that moment, there was only me and her. I ran full speed into her arms. It felt like I was home again. Except for a few scars and an eye that opened slightly less wide than its counterpart, I appeared perfectly normal.

After a full day at the hospital, we piled back into Mr. Williams' Mercedes. He dropped us off at the hotel to freshen up, and said he would return to pick us up for dinner to celebrate a successful day. Jerline put Crystal down for a nap to compensate for her uprooted schedule while we changed into something more suitable for an elaborate dinner out. Before too long, I was in the backseat of the Mercedes again.

The restaurant was truly fancy. They had white linen tablecloths and matching napkins. Ice water was served in goblets, each place setting had two forks, and each table had a candle. I read through the menu and saw several meals that were unfamiliar. I spotted the veal Parmesan and thought that it sounded sufficiently fancy. I wanted a fancy dinner. When I noticed the veal was $14.95, I announced that it was too much, and that I'd select something else. Mr. Williams leaned over and patiently explained that it was rude to comment on the cost of a meal when someone else was treating. Not wanting to be rude, I went ahead and ordered the veal. Our dinner salads came, then the entrees.

Several bites in, Mr. Williams asked me if I was enjoying my meal. "Mmm, yes—it's really good. What is veal anyway?" I asked.

"It's a baby cow. That's why it's so tender," Mr. Williams explained matter-of-factly.

"It's…it's what?!" I asked, certain I'd misunderstood what he said. For the second time that day, I had a flashback. This time I was transported to the pasture behind our house in Florida. I remembered meeting Bessie for the first time, bonding with her through the fence, hand-feeding her, feeling her velvety nose on my hand, and watching her birth Betsy. I was there when she was born, I watched her stand for the first time and take her first wobbly steps, I listened as she found her voice, and I even named her. All of a sudden I lost my appetite. I couldn't take another bite if my life depended on it.

My visit to Philadelphia came to an end, and it was time to head back to the warmth of Florida, my brothers, and the rest of the Lariscy family. I reflected on all that I had done and seen during this brief visit: being a guest in a fancy hotel, returning to the hospital where I spent four weeks recovering after the near-fatal accident, and learning some nuances of social skills. Even though I didn't realize it at the time, I was so fortunate that Mr. Williams was there to represent and defend my best interests where the lawsuit was concerned, the same way the Lariscys looked after my best interests in matters of day-to-day life. It really does take a village.

Within a week or so after returning from Philadelphia, we learned that Dad was working hard to reclaim us and we would soon be moving back to Ohio. While I was distraught at the notion of leaving the Lariscys, I was excited to be able to pick up where I'd left off with Dad. He was always by far my favorite parent and the only one I missed. I had fond memories of dancing and acting silly with him. My excitement was compounded when I realized that we'd be living in Waynesville, the same town as Aunt Mary and Andy. This meant we'd be able to see Andy again. And the same way a cherry makes a hot fudge sundae better, I also expected that Dad's promise from five years earlier would be realized: we'd be able to get Gayle back. That, after all, was the plan when Grandma's cousins took her away.

The last week of school before Christmas break, I could feel my emotions churn as I said goodbye to my friends and told them that I wouldn't be returning after the New Year. We celebrated Christmas with the Lariscys before leaving for Ohio. The gifts we received were wonderful, but the best gift of all was the fact that we were going to be a family again. Emotions ran deep as we said our goodbyes. As excited as I was to be reunited with Dad, I was equally distressed to be leaving the Lariscys. I had only been with them for a year and a half, but it was a fundamental time of growth for me. I had many new experiences that lent normalcy to my life.

The day had arrived, and my heart was shattered. At one point in the not-too-distant past, I'd wanted nothing more than to leave the Lariscys behind. Now, as we were saying our final goodbyes,

I felt like life could not go on without them. For all intents and purposes, Jerline was my mother, which meant she was my coach, my therapist, my biggest fan, my strongest advocate, and my role model. She was the mother I always wanted but never had, and even more than that, she was my guardian angel. I cried like I'd never cried before; every cell in my body, it seemed, cried with me. I wrapped my arms around Jerline and clung to her as if my life depended on it. I wouldn't, couldn't let go.

As if communication between my brain and arms had ceased, my body knew that I needed to let go but my heart and soul refused. Jerline hugged me back, matching my intensity. I could feel her sorrow as well, but in typical Jerline fashion, she marshalled all of her strength and found a way to mother me one last time. "Hey, hey, hey," she said as she cupped my chin with her perfectly manicured hands. She lifted my head to look into my eyes the way mothers do when they really need to get their point across. But I couldn't see her face through my swollen eyes that were flooded with tears. Even still, I instinctively knew that tender maternal look she was giving me. "If you ever need me, honey, I'm only a phone call away."

In memory of Henry Lariscy Sr. and Alan D. Williams Jr., Esq.
I wish you were still here to see that your sacrifices weren't in vain.
Thank you for being so selfless.

Dumpster Doll: Adolescence
AN EXCERPT FROM BOOK TWO

A nd just like that, we were on our way. In the span of less than a month, I was on the second flight of my life. I used the flight time to process my feelings about leaving the Lariscys, leaving the friends I had made at school, and leaving Jerline. On one hand, life was turning upside down—again—but on the other hand, I was ecstatic about reuniting with Dad. How could this be anything but wonderful? My mind was flooded with fond memories of dancing with Dad in the living room to Bob Seger songs and Dad goofing off like a caveman during the Ally Oop song. Oh, how I wished the plane would fly faster to get us to Ohio sooner.

After a few hours, we landed at the airport in Dayton, Ohio, where Dad met us. "Dad! DAAAAD!" I ran up and gave him a big hug as soon as I spotted him through the sea of holiday travelers.

To BE CONTINUED...

Acknowledgments

We wish to extend our gratitude to our beta readers. Your feedback and support have helped in so many ways:

Dr. Kimberly Carter, Dr. Diane Kline, Laura Clark, Audrey O'Brien, Nancy Luce, Katherine Shanahan, Brian Luce, Paulette O'Brien, Lynn West, Marty Khudairi, Natalie Payne, Kimberly Schroeder, Tim Klugh, Lori Klugh, Duane Robinson, Beth Robinson, Bridget Febus, Barb Roland, Barbara Moone, Nick Kweckel, Nick Singh, Linda Brutger, Monica Dalzell, Kate Taylor Clewell, Mary Thompson, Linda Thompson, Barb Dumas, John Isaacs, Andy Thompson, Lisa Thompson, Gayle Cabello, Niderra Malone, Tameisha Daniels, Michelle McCrory, Rachel Mortman, Cindy Crum, Hanna Organ, Rhonda Chamberlain, Ted Wood, Donna Wood, Kristina Sprinkles, Mia Tagano, LeeAnn Phillips, Joseph Woodward, Mike Berardi, Nora Berardi, Tricia Sherwood,

Dianna Carter, Julia Neville, Jerline Hendrix, Crystal Morgan, Randy Lariscy, Amanda Lariscy, Jeanie Lariscy, Scott Mays, Brandon Lewis, Brent Lewis, Tyler Mays, Samantha Lewis, Amanda McGheehan, Kevin Earp, and Regina Starkey-Beeler.

SPECIAL THANKS

Dr. Diana Kline, thank you so much for the push and motivation to begin this book and for helping so much with the editing, beta reading, and encouragement along the way. You are truly an inspiration to many young women and a wonderful friend.

Brad, Heather, and Emily of Columbus Publishing Lab, thank you so much for having such a wonderful outlet for a set of new authors such as us and being so open with your professional knowledge and expertise to help us present *Dumpster Doll: The Early Years* in the best possible light. Brad, you set us straight with your seminar from the get-go on how publishing works; if not for you, we would still be waiting on a "Big 5" publisher, which may have never happened. Heather, you forced us to expand our knowledge of taking a story from good to excellent. Emily, your encouragement and work with us has meant so much. I'm still taking you up on that margarita offer. We look forward to working with you on the next two books.

Ryan Elmiger, thank you for your enthusiastic assistance with fresh marketing ideas. We greatly value your experience and wisdom.

Special Acknowledgments From Michelle Mays

To my husband, Scott, thank you for putting up with the long nights when I was absent while working on this. Also thank you for balancing me out where needed to make me stronger. I know I am not always at my best, and the fact that you stuck around through those times shows your love for me. You have been a great partner and father. I love you.

To my children, Brandon, Brent, and Tyler, you don't know how much you all saved my life by motivating me to be a good person and mother. We pretty much grew up together. I hope I didn't screw you up in my learning process. I am so proud of the men that you have become. Mommy loves you!

To my bestie in the whole wide world, Michelle Moone (my co-author), I am so glad you were laid off so we could start this journey together. Who knew what a great outcome would result from such sad events? I couldn't have opened up to anyone else the way I have to you. Thank you so much for making it easy to reveal such personal moments and not judging me for it. You are a beautiful person inside and out. I love you bunches!

SPECIAL ACKNOWLEDGMENTS
FROM MICHELLE MOONE

To my family and friends—Dad, Marty, Frank, Beth, Barbara, Nick, Natalie, Jen, Karim, and Linda—thank you for believing in me and this book. Your encouragement, support, and cheers helped me when I ran dry. Thank you for your willingness to always offer suitable distractions when I needed sanity breaks, even if you never realized I was using you for this purpose.

Mom, how I wish you were here to see this; I know you're watching down on me, and I hope I've made you proud.

Maggie and Izzie, thank you for patiently waiting for your walks, then traipsing along on extra long walks while I worked out how to best convey emotion and intent, especially in some of the more difficult chapters.

To Michelle Mays, my best friend and little sister, the dumpster doll—I love you! Your friendship means the world to me and I love that we both have September birthdays so we can Michelle-abrate together. I so admire your strength and character and I am in awe of your willingness to share such personal tragedy and inspire greatness. Thank you for letting me write your memoir; I look forward to the next two books.

Deep gratitude to God who sent his best guardian angels—some heavenly and some earthbound—to watch over Michelle and make sure she survived her heartbreaking childhood. He set us out on different paths, but in His infinite wisdom, He allowed our paths to cross.

A HUGE thank you to anyone who purchased this book. We hope it helps open your eyes and hearts to the many traumas that children endure all over this great country. Let's make a difference in a child's life and give them some positive memories!

—The Michelles

If you would like to donate your time or money to help foster children and make a difference in their lives, here are two very worthy organizations that are dedicated to the betterment of the circumstances of foster children.

CASA (Court Appointed Special Advocates)
www.casaforchildren.org

Dave Thomas Foundation for Adoption
www.davethomasfoundation.org

CPSIA information can be obtained
at www.ICGtesting.com
Printed in the USA
FFHW021455150120
57822316-63089FF

9 781633 373389